S0-ATW-138

9/23/08

MOBILIZING

THE GREEN REVOLUTION

TO: JULIA WHITTY,

WHAT I THINK
YOU MIGHT ENJOY.

BEST REGARDS,

C. King...

MOBILIZING
THE GREEN REVOLUTION
Money and Manpower to Save the Planet

John C. Krieg

www.ivyhousebooks.com

PUBLISHED BY IVY HOUSE PUBLISHING GROUP
5122 Bur Oak Circle, Raleigh, NC 27612
United States of America
919-782-0281
www.ivyhousebooks.com

ISBN: 1-57197-468-7
Library of Congress Control Number: 2006903407

© 2006 John C. Krieg
All rights reserved, which includes the right to reproduce
this book or portions thereof in any form whatsoever except
as provided by the U.S. Copyright Law.

Printed in the United States of America

*To my uncle/father figure Vernon W. Rounds.
He moved like a shadow in the woods and
never killed an animal that wasn't thoroughly
used. He taught me his love of nature and
all things natural.*

Other Books by John C. Krieg

Desert Landscape Architecture, 1999
Environmental Cognizance, 2005
Econation, 2006
Career in Crisis, Coming in early 2007
Ravings from the High Chaparral, Coming in late 2007

Contents

1933–1942) and the Peace Corps as models for a modern day Environmental Corps.

Examines the current state of America's prison and juvenile detention systems. Explains why there must be a national paradigm shift in how offenders are dealt with. Looks into a social epidemic that is sweeping the youth of our country—home schooling.

Examines why the environmental movement represents the new job frontier. As the American national attitude becomes more receptive to environmental causes, new jobs will present themselves in the areas of restoration, monitoring, and management.

Examines the idea of creating a "patchwork quilt" of donated private properties that can be utilized for habitat restoration. Studies the Nature Conservancy's and Trust for Public Land's methods of acquiring and managing land. Explores green investment opportunities.

Briefly discusses the history of cities and why things have gone awry. Studies the revitalization of existing urban areas as it relates to the coming human stampede back to the cities.

By using the Declaration of Independence and the US
Constitution as jumping off points, an argument is made
that the current citizenry of America can pressure its leaders to legislate clean air and clean water as an inalienable
right. Worries that the environmental cause is often not
without peril.

Revisits the development fate of the rural southern
California town of Anza, which was written about in the
Epilogue of *Econation*. Examines the development history
and emerging development opportunities at the Salton
Sea–California's largest lake.

Works Cited

1. *How Foundations Work: What Grantseekers Need to Know About The Many Faces of Foundations.*
   Dennis P. McIlnay.
   San Francisco: Jossey-Bass, a Wiley Imprint, 1998.

2. *Winning Grants Step by Step.*
   Mim Carlson.
   San Francisco: Jossey-Bass, a Wiley Imprint, 2002.

3. *Demystifying Grant Seeking: What You Really Need to Do to Get Grants.* Second Edition.
   Larissa Golden Brown & Martin John Brown.
   San Francisco: Jossey-Bass, a Wiley Imprint, 2001.

4. *American Foundations: An Investigative History.*
   Mark Dowie.
   Cambridge: The MIT Press, 2001.

5. *The Seven Faces of Philanthropy: A New Approach to Cultivating Major Donors.*
   Russ Alan Prince & Karen Maru File.

San Francisco: Jossey-Bass, a Wiley Imprint, 1994.

6. *Beyond Fund Raising: New Strategies for Nonprofit Innovation and Investment.*
   Kay Sprinkel Grace.
   New York: John Wiley & Sons, Inc., 1997.

7. *Fundraising Fundamentals: A Guide to Annual Giving for Professionals and Volunteers.* Second Edition.
   James M. Greenfield.
   New York: John Wiley & Sons, Inc., 2002.

8. *The CCC Chronicles: Camp Newspapers of the Civilian Conservation Corps, 1933–1942.*
   Alfred Emile Cornebise.
   Jefferson: McFarland & Company Inc., Publishers, 2004.

9. *So, You Want to Join the Peace Corps: What to Know Before You Go.*
   Dillon Banerjee.
   Berkeley: Ten Speed Press, 2000.

10. *Megatrends and Volunteerism: Mapping the Future of Volunteer Programs.*
    Sue Vineyard.
    Heritage Arts Publishing, 1993.

11. *Promises Betrayed: Waking Up From The American Dream.*
    Bob Herbert.
    New York: Times Books
    Henry Holt and Company, LLC, 2005.

12. *The Conscription Society: Administered Mass Organizations.*
Gregory J. Kasza.
New Haven: Yale University Press, 1995.

13. *Changing the Lawbreaker: The Treatment of Delinquents and Criminals.*
Don C. Gibbons.
Montclair: Allanheld, Osmun & Co. Publishers, Inc., 1981.

14. *Making Sense With Offenders: Personal Constructs, Therapy and Change.*
Julia Huston.
West Sussex: John Wiley & Sons, Ltd., 1998.

15. *Design with Nature: 25th Anniversary Edition.*
Ian L. McHarg.
New York: John Wiley & Sons, Inc., 1992.

16. *Eco-Pioneers: Practical Visionaries Solving Today's Environmental Problems.*
Steve Lerner.
Cambridge: The MIT Press, 1997.

17. *Vital Signs 2005: The Trends That Are Shaping Our Future.*
The Worldwatch Institute. Lisa Mastny, Project Director.
New York: W.W. Norton & Company, Inc., 2005.

18. *The Consumer's Guide to Effective Environmental Choices: Practical Advice from the Union of Concerned Scientists.*

Michael Brower, Ph.D. & Warren Leon, Ph.D.
New York: Three Rivers Press, 1999.

19. *The Sacred Balance: Rediscovering Our Place in Nature.*
David Suzuki with Amanda McConnell.
Vancouver, B.C.: Greystone Books, 2002.

20. *Environmental Cognizance: Towards The Year 2020.*
John C. Krieg.
Raleigh: Ivy House Publishing Group, 2005.

21. *President Theodore Roosevelt's Conservation Legacy.*
W. Todd Benson.
Haverford: Infinity Publishing.com, 2003.

22. *Wild Card Quilt: Taking A Chance On Home.*
Janisse Ray.
Minneapolis: Milkweed Editions, 2003.

23. *Continental Conservation: Scientific Foundations of Regional Reserve Networks.*
Michael E. Soule & John Terborgh, Editors.
Washington: Island Press, 1999.

24. *Land Trust Standards and Practices.*
Washington: Land Trust Alliance, 2004.

25. *The City in History: Its Origins, Its Transformations, and Its Prospects.*
Lewis Mumford.
Orlando: Harcourt, Inc., 1961.

26. *Cities.* Second Edition.
Lawrence Halprin.
Cambridge: The MIT Press, 1972.

27. *Cities Back from the Edge: New Life for Downtown.*
Roberta Brandes Grantz with Norman Mintz.
John Wiley & Sons, Inc., 1998.

28. *The Experience of Place: New Ways of Looking at and Dealing with our Radically Changing Cities and Countryside.*
Tony Hiss.
New York: Vintage Books, 1990.

29. *The Geography of Nowhere: The Rise and Decline of America's Man-Made Landscape.*
James Howard Kunstler.
New York: Touchstone, 1993.

30. *The Next American Metropolis: Ecology, Community, and the American Dream.*
Peter Calthorpe.
New York: Princeton Architectural Press, 1993.

31. *The Great Work: Our Way into the Future.*
Thomas Berry.
New York: Bell Tower, 1999.

32. *The Long Emergency: Surviving the Converging Catastrophes of the Twenty-First Century.*
James Howard Kunstler.
Grove/Atlantic, Inc., 2005.

33. *The Declaration of Independence.*
Action of Second Continental Congress.
July 4th, 1776.

34. *The Riverkeepers: Two Activists Fight to Reclaim our Environment as a Basic Human Right.*
John Cronin & Robert F. Kennedy, Jr.
New York: Touchstone, 1997.

35. *Losing Ground: American Environmentalism at the Close of the Twentieth Century.*
Mark Dowie.
Cambridge: The MIT Press, 1995.

36. *The War Against the Greens: The "Wise-Use" Movement, the New Right and the Browning of America.* Revised Edition.
David Helvarg.
Boulder: Johnson Books, 2004.

37. *Earthjustice Website.*
earthjustice.org, 2005.

38. *America's Environmental Report Card: Are We Making the Grade?*
Harvey Blatt.
Cambridge: The MIT Press, 2004.

39. *Human Nature: A Blueprint for Managing the Earth— by People, for People.*
James Trefil.
New York: Times Books, 2004.

40. *The Living Bible.* et al.
    Wheaton: Tyndale House Publishers, 1978.

41. *Nature-Friendly Communities: Habitat Protection and Land Use Planning.*
    Christopher Duerksen & Cara Snyder.
    Washington D.C.: Island Press, 2005.

42. *Salt Dreams: Land & Water in Low-Down California.*
    William deBuys & Joan Myers.
    Albuquerque: University of New Mexico Press, 1999.

43. *The High Country Journal: Your Local Newspaper for Anza & Aguanga.*
    Vicki Conover.
    May 1st, June 1st, June 15th, 2005 Editions.

Songs Quoted

a. "Money": *Dark Side of the Moon*
   Pink Floyd, 1973

b. "Court and Spark": *Court and Spark*
   Joni Mitchell, 1974

c. "The Spider and the Fly": *Out of Our Heads*
   The Rolling Stones, 1965

d. "Come From the Heart": *Traces*
   Richard Leigh & Susanna Clark, 1987

e. "Lord, Have Mercy on the Working Man": *T-R-O-U-B-L-E*
   Travis Tritt, 1992

f. "The Beat Goes On": *In Case You're in Love*
   Sonny & Cher, 1967

Prelude

My basic concept is to reach the common man with the simple message that he does count and he can make a difference. All these environmental organizations and societies are fine although there seems to me to be a lot of back patting, bordering on outright snobbery, among many of their members. There is an element of intellectual one-upmanship within the environmental movement that's limiting its growth or hastening its demise—take your pick. In either case, the exclusiveness of a club limits its membership. This is good if you're a fraternity or sorority trying to hoard all the good looking people on campus and not so good if you're trying to get a revolution off the ground. A common theme among environmentalists is that the movement has lost momentum since its zenith in the seventies. While this is true it misses the more important point, which is to define what momentum really is.

In *Environmental Cognizance* I wrote that momentum comes from action and not the other way around. I steadfastly stand by these words but feel I owe it to the readership to define what action is. Simply put, the environmental crisis needs to be attacked on the two fronts of money and manpower.

Money isn't everything; it's the one thing that will restore the planet. How it's procured is practically more important than how it is utilized, for money that funds projects establishes a momentum all its own, which is known as cash flow. Good cash flow can and often does hide a multitude of organizational and managerial sins. While it would be nice to be one hundred percent efficient in the utilization of acquired funds, it's next to impossible in a movement where there are hundreds, perhaps thousands, of disjointed yet well-meaning organizations. The first priority of funds procurement is to pay salaries, offset overhead, and insure the survival of the organization. Environmental programs, endowments, awards, and such get what's left and if these are ill-thought out or mismanaged, the environment ultimately suffers. But without the efforts of these organizations and the exposure they bring to the environmental crisis, how much worse off would the environment be? The cash flow juggernaut must continue to rattle and shake and stumble and bumble along if we are to harbor any hope at all for saving the planet.

The overall scope of the planetary environmental problems are so enormous that all the money in the world, in and of itself, wouldn't be enough to put a dent in them. Manpower must be made available either through volunteerism or conscription and the payoff must be in something other than dollars, which there are not enough of anyway. Educational advancement, personal satisfaction, freedom from confinement, or relief from incarceration must be used in lieu of salaries.

In defining a course of action the cart has always been in front of the horse in the environmental movement and this is its biggest shortcoming. A recognition of the problem, unless one is blind, illiterate, insensitive, or extremely stupid, is no great achievement. Environmental degradation screams at us in every sensory dimension. Scientists have adopted a "tip of the iceberg" proclamation, stating that what we don't know is probably far worse than what we do. Immobilized by fear, the general public shuts down. With these issues out of sight, out of mind, the general populace concentrates on its everyday work life and pressing social issues, which is a mystery to me because they are far more severe than any environmental problem. The species man concentrates on accommodating an organism (itself) that is growing completely out of control, while at the same time ignoring the health of the system upon which it sustains and nourishes itself. This is the plight of the parasite. What will it do when the host finally dies?

Defining the scope of the work to be done is a daunting task in light of a constantly changing landscape. Just about the time every problem receives a file number, one thousand more appear, and the office filing system needs more cabinets and when they arrive there isn't enough floor space so you have to expand to another floor and after the tenant improvements the building collapses under the increased weight. When the dust finally settles you realize you don't even know the true scope of the problems, and what's worse, you haven't even started to work on the first one. Just about the time the rent bill arrives and the insurance carrier goes belly up you realize that you would have been better off working on a few of the problems rather than trying to corral them all. Somewhere inherent in defining the scope of work comes the survival mechanism known as the division of labor.

While various environmental organizations bicker back and forth over who is going to do what, it might be a good idea to attempt to slow the rate of the earth's despoliation so there's a planet left to rescue after the work orders are handed out and the purchase vouchers get delivered.

I'm frequently reminded of the popular television commercial where the corporate executive states that amidst all the problem quantifiers in his organization he would gladly kill for one good solution to just one problem. We can only hope that he starts by killing all the whiners that surround him. It's the one good solution that we need to concern ourselves with. One down with one hundred to go may not seem too terribly encouraging but it's still one down.

At best, the green revolution has stagnated and at worst, to quote investigative environmental writer Mark Dowie, it's "losing ground." Although it oftentimes attracts glamorous people it is not a particularly glamorous movement. This is not a romanticized version of a Pancho Villa-style uprising, it's test tubes and microscopes and scientific papers produced by mild mannered people who lack charisma and are no slave to fashion.

It's a strange irony that television networks are producing a glut of investigative forensic science cop shows basically stating that it's becoming progressively harder and harder to get away with killing someone. At the same time nature's forensic scientists are witnessing and proving the murder of planet earth with hardly a spark of interest from the general public. Seems like sinister death trumps slow death in the entertainment department. Or perhaps it's the sense of closure that grabs us. On the cop show the killer(s) are found out and brought to justice while on the earth's big screen it's hard to write an episode where we arrest ourselves.

So how does excitement get infused into something as mundane as global destruction? How do we make environmental careers more alluring? How do we define new frontiers that are as exciting as the Old West or the space race? How do we impress upon the general populace the severity of the situation? It has to be couched in terms of life or death or it won't get much play. This is why those cop shows are so popular—something (the thing most precious to us all) is at risk. Many people, myself sometimes included, state openly that they will be long gone before the final curtain is drawn on planet earth, so why bother? When you leave an apartment you clean the place up to get your security deposit back. You have a vested interest that compels you to tidy up, but is this the sole reason why you perform the task? Does not a part of you feel responsible for the wear and tear you have inflicted upon the unit? Do you not want to send a message to the landlord that you're a decent, responsible, clean, and caring person?

Your actions may be driven seventy percent for the refund and thirty percent for the self-respect. Not too surprisingly, it's within the lower percentage of your motivation where the future of the earth lies. Think of future generations as the landlord you never met but who will ultimately hold you accountable. Sure, you can move to another state and dodge those nasty collection notices but at the end of the day you have to ask yourself, "Am I that kind of person?"

Leaving the earth better than when you came takes a lifetime commitment. Aldo Leopold spoke of a conservation ethic, but it was just a concept in the forties. Sixty years later it still hasn't came to fruition. One has to wonder what it will take to put the health of the planet first in everyone's mind; from who or what will spring a sense of urgency? Nature has to become fundamentally and monumentally important to us. It has to mean what driving out a monarchy meant to Washington. What repealing slavery meant to Lincoln. What stopping Custer meant to Sitting Bull. What eradicating Nazis meant to Churchill. What human rights meant to Kennedy and Martin Luther King. What tracking down Bin Laden means to the Bushes. What supporting your children means to you. It means working to succeed despite the costs, as failure is not an option.

When we can finally see the writing on the wall that the life of the planet rests in our hands then perhaps we can make meaningful plans for its future. This isn't a national debt we can pass on to future generations without too much guilt because we know that they can do the same if they so choose. This is an inevitable extinction unless we reverse earth-destructive, which is to say self-destructive, trends.

Chapter One: Quotes
Grant Writing and Management

Foundations are mysterious, and they are poorly understood even by the people in nonprofit organizations that receive grants from them. They play an important role in society but remain remarkably unknown and unstudied. Few books on foundations are analytical. Most are descriptive and anecdotal, relying on "war stories" but little or no research. Many others are quantitative, reciting numbers, types, assets, and grants; from this information we do gain some understanding of foundations' basic characteristics, but we still do not grasp their more substantive features and we know next to nothing about what goes on inside them.[1]

How Foundations Work
Dennis P. McIlney

There is no mystery to writing a successful proposal. The keys to success are:

Developing a clear program plan
Researching funders thoroughly
Building a strong relationship with funders
Targeting your proposals carefully
Writing a concise proposal [2]

Winning Grants: Step by Step
Mim Carlson

Myth: Grants are something for nothing
Reality: Grants are rational deals between colleagues . . .
Grants are appealing because they look like big chunks of free money. Unlike most individual donations, grants are often large enough to actually buy something, that is, to fund a whole program for an entire year or to purchase a major piece of equipment. And to get a grant you just send in an application. The funder sends back a check, and you don't need to pay it back. A grant seems like manna from heaven or a winning lottery ticket. . . . Grants are not free money. Foundations and

1

other grant makers are organizations like your nonprofit. They have missions and goals just as you do. Funders award grants because what the grant recipients plan to do with the money fits in with the funders' own goals, initiatives, and dreams—and with their founder's stated wishes.[3]

Demystifying Grant Seeking
Larissa Golden Brown and John Martin Brown

The bottom line of the reforms I propose (back to real economics!) is that maintaining the present structure of organized philanthropy makes a certain amount of sense—moral as well as economic sense. It is true that the wealth of foundations, profits accumulated by the capitalist class, remains invested, albeit generally in land and securities and not necessarily in productive capacity, and that all too often it is used to advance enterprises that are dissonant with a foundation's declared purpose. Still, rather than liquidating all that wealth—along with the opportunity to use it for genuinely progressive philanthropy—would it not be sensible to encourage the formation of more democratic foundations, to tax the incomes of the uncharitable rich more heavily, and to transfer the funds collected (not the foundations' stocks, bonds, and real estate) directly to the neediest?[4]

American Foundations: An Investigative History
Mark Dowie

Money, it's a hit.
Don't give me that do goody good bullshit![a]

Pink Floyd's "Money"

Chapter One

Grant Writing and Management

Money. Everybody wants it. Few people have it, or very much of it anyway. Although some say it's the root of all evil they also realize that without it, freedom—at least the best freedom, financial freedom—would be impossible. So, herein lies the problem; how does money protect one's freedom without corrupting one's ethics? While few believe that anyone could have too much money, many know the hardships brought about by not having enough. Whether too much or not enough, there is one common denominator to money. Everybody wants it.

Ninety percent of all the wealth in America is hoarded by less than ten percent of the citizenry. The disparity in living conditions and access to services between the super-rich and the very poor is represented by a wide chasm. The rich say the poor are too lazy and irresponsible to get ahead while the poor say that the rich won't let them. The truth, as it usually does, lies somewhere in the middle. And in terms of wealth, most people feel that the answer lies exactly in the middle. If only the rich had less, the poor could have more, and equality would be achieved among mankind. Pull the economic bar down for the former and up for the latter. This socialistic view has never gone over in America, where the capitalistic rule most frequently applied is that each gets their own on their own merits. Dog eat dog, in other words.

Some dogs have indeed eaten very well. Andrew Carnegie was born dirt poor in Scotland in 1835. He immigrated to the United States in 1848 at age thirteen. He began working (immigrants were always working) in cotton mills and telegraph offices, and eventually hooked on with the Pennsylvania Railroad. He introduced the first Pullman sleeping car in 1859, which earned him a promotion to head of the western division. Carnegie recognized the importance of steel in America's emerging industrial revolution and resigned from the railroad in 1865 to form the Keystone Bridge Company. He quickly acquired other holdings that provided steel rails for the nation's rapidly expanding railroad system. Carnegie worked at a tireless, frantic pace for thirty-six years and then sold his holdings lock, stock, and barrel to J. P. Morgan in 1901.

Perhaps because it was the dawn of a new century, perhaps because he could see his own mortality staring back at him in the mirror, perhaps because of divine intervention, Carnegie became this country's greatest philanthropist and literally gave away over 350 million dollars over the next eighteen years until his death in 1919. Carnegie and his money were the driving forces behind the nation's library system and 2,500 separate facilities were built as a direct result of his efforts. It should be noted that even this huge sum of money (really huge by 1900s standards) didn't fund everything. Carnegie put the infrastructure in place, but it was up to communities and their respective governments to fund the procurement of books and staff the facilities. This is key in understanding the true nature of philanthropy. Rarely can a donation or endowment fund a need kit and caboodle. This initial seed, or start-up money, simply gets the ball rolling. Then it is up to the efforts of others to keep it moving.

John Davison Rockefeller's life and eventual philanthropic vision parallels Carnegie's. Born in 1839, he lived to the ripe old age of ninety-eight. Founder of Standard Oil in 1870, he amassed many holdings and a vast fortune, eventually becoming America's first billionaire. His oil empire was broken up into thirty-nine separate holdings in 1911 when the US Supreme Court ruled that he was running a monopoly in violation of the Sherman Anti-Trust Act. He then turned his considerable energies to founding the Rockefeller Foundation with the mandate, "To promote the well-being of mankind throughout the world." It's estimated that Rockefeller contributed at least half his fortune to this foundation.

Henry Ford was born in 1863. Basically uneducated, he was a self-made man with an aptitude of genius proportions for mechanics. He escaped the rigors of farm life at age fifteen and trained as a machinist in Detroit, Michigan. He began experiments on a horseless carriage in 1890 and by 1896 introduced the quadricycle, which was powered by a two-cylinder gasoline engine. The rest, as they say, is history. Ford's automotive facility went through a boom period with the Model T, followed by a bust period due to unrelenting old-style management practices. Although he never relinquished total control, he did turn over the reigns to his only son, Edsel, in 1919. Ford automotive experienced a rebirth with the introduction of the Model A in 1928 and the subsequent production of the V-8 engine. Henry Ford established the Ford Foundation in 1936 with the broad mission statement, "To serve the nation's general welfare." He and Edsel poured large portions of their personal fortunes into this foundation throughout their lives, with Edsel dying in 1943, and Henry in 1947. Today, the Ford Foundation is the largest philanthropic giver in America.

Carnegie, Rockefeller, and Ford were the true pioneers of the foundation movement in the United States. Carnegie, Ford, and Rockefeller, to a lesser degree, placed a huge premium on the education of the masses, of which many would join the work forces of their (and their successors) various plants and factories when they came of working age. Thus, it can be said that some of their charity was self-serving and business perpetuating. Whatever means serves the end, say I. Without these three, and others to follow, education in America would have been in dire straights, especially for the "lower" classes.

Foundations initially received tax-exempt status from the federal government which, for sixty-eight out of their first one hundred years of existence, caused them to be viewed and criticized as glorified tax-dodges. This perception was magnified in the early days of foundation creation, as the founder's children and other family members frequently populated any given foundation's board of directors. This nepotism, resulting in high salaries paid for work that frequently garnered dubious results, heightened the public's sense of general distrust.

While the structure of foundations frequently mimics the structure of the corporations (or the corporate founder) that created them, the comparison stops here. For the most part, foundations operate with impunity, free from the threat of anti-trust suits, charges of income tax-evasion, and public or private claims of mismanagement or ineptitude. Those most likely to call them into account are those who were most likely turned down for a grant request, and there is nothing Americans hate more than a sore loser. Until quite recently, the foundation business centered on two known entities—

grant makers and grant seekers—those who had the money and those that wanted it. Unfortunately, by some accounts, this degenerated into beggars and those that passed judgment on the worthiness of the beggars, and as everyone knows, beggars can't be choosers.

The last thing in the world a beggar would do is criticize the one person (foundation) who he is begging to until he knows, for a fact, that he isn't going to get what he's begging for. From the early days of the 1900s until they came under investigation in the sixties, foundations existed much the way the Catholic Church existed in the dark Middle Ages. Their authority went unchallenged although everyone suspected that on some level, perhaps many levels, they were corrupt.

The congressional investigation of the sixties culminated in the Tax Reform Act of 1969, which subjected foundations to a four percent tax on their investment income, which was reduced to two percent in 1978.

It's difficult to ascertain whether this helped or hurt grant seekers. On the surface, it seems unquestionable that it hurt them because the argument can be made that through taxation the federal government cut into the foundation's disposable income, making less available to those perceived to really need it. Things are not always what they seem to be however, and the more meaningful outcome was that the overall assets of any given foundation became known, and those bogarting the mother lode were exposed. Cracks began to appear on the ironclad walls of foundations that had heretofore seemed impenetrable.

It's generally felt that foundations, by necessity, must survive. Here again, they can be likened to corporations. To facilitate this end they usually invest in reliable real estate stocks, bonds, and other low-risk investments, slowly amass a portfolio of wealth, and operate and give from the interest accrued. Of the trillions that foundations reflect in combined net worth, typically only five percent of annual profits is given out as grants and endowments.

In *American Foundations: An Investigative History,* noted environmental journalist Mark Dowie questioned the survivability of foundations as an absolute given, questioned the continuing stand-offishness of many foundations, questioned everything. Quite simply, the man is one hell of a reporter.

Dowie cites as an example of an antithesis to the survivability theory the story of Irene Diamond, a woman who deserves the status of a true American hero. Her husband, Aaron Diamond, a New York real estate mogul of sometimes questionable ethics, died unexpectedly of a heart attack in 1984. Associates tried to pressure her into signing legal papers before his body turned cold. Mrs. Diamond held firm and sought out the advice of W. H. Ferry, a well-known philanthropist who had extensive experience and involvement with the Ford Foundation. Ferry advised her not to sign the documents, which, not too surprisingly, would have had her relinquish all control of her husband's assets. She was then introduced to Vincent McGee, who was entrusted with the responsibility of setting up a foundation that could preserve the interests she had shared with her deceased husband—human rights, medical research, and the advancement of education. She soon became aware of a problem that is all too typical to far too many foundations. It became obvious to Mrs. Diamond that the board being assembled to carry out her deceased husband's wishes was more interested in their own. They wanted her participation to be minimal and they were dead set on creating a foundation that advanced their interests, not to mention their salaries.

Dead men tell no tales. They also can't tell whether or not their wishes are carried out after they're dead. It's up to the living to protect them. Irene Diamond wasn't going to stand for being pushed to the side. Amidst all the shenanigans that were going on, she hit upon what it was that she really wanted to do, which was to utilize the foundation to *make a difference during her lifetime*. Irene Diamond came to the conclusion that all the assets of the foundation would be spent within ten years and the foundation subsequently dissolved.

Of roughly 250 million dollars in assets, the foundation would spend 25 million a year. Before his death, her husband had stated he wanted twenty percent spent on cultural pursuits, forty percent on minority education, and forty percent on medical research. In the area of medical research, Irene Diamond most firmly took hold of the reigns and targeted AIDS research as her number one priority. The foundation began operation in 1987 just as the AIDS epidemic in New York City began to approach crisis proportions. AIDS was an issue that most staunchly conservative foundations chose to avoid, while the federal government characteristically looked the other way. Diamond funded thirty research programs nationwide and opened the Aaron Diamond AIDS Research Center in 1990. Dr. David Ho was appointed its director and was named *Time Magazine's* Man of the Year in 1996. Under Dr. Ho, the center was able to find a way to suppress the disease in newborns and alleviate suffering among adults.

By making the altruistic decision to "spend out" her foundation, Irene Diamond was able to pump huge infusions of cash into research of a disease at a time when there was a small window of opportunity to repress it before it became an epidemic in the United States. Call it luck if you will, for her timing turned out to be impeccable, but it is a provable fact that those that aggressively pursue their aspirations frequently do get lucky. Thousands of people owe their lives to the direct efforts and unwavering courage of Irene Diamond, a woman who did indeed make a difference in her own lifetime.

After the government's shakeup of foundations in 1969, one would think that their numbers would have declined. Nothing could be further from the truth. After a momentary blip on their radar screen, the number of American foundations began to grow at an astounding rate. Upon looking around at other opportunities, new founders quickly discovered that forming a foundation was still the best vehicle for sheltering acquired wealth, giving your ne'er-do-well kids a real job, and seeing that your philanthropic wishes, while living, were carried out while dead.

The demographics of America reveal that the babies of the baby boom are all reaching retirement age *now*. Forty percent of the nation's population will retire from active participation in the work force within the next ten years. Those lucky enough to become super-rich will attempt to shelter their wealth in foundations, where it's estimated that twenty percent of the total transfer of wealth—trillions—will wind up in foundations whose endowments will fund the aspirations of contemporaries of their children and grandchildren.

For every foundation, there are at least twenty nonprofit grant seeking organizations that could desperately use their money and this ratio is disproportionately increasing on the grant seekers' side.

Today there are over fifty thousand foundations in America. The broad based percentages of what foundations fund break down like this:

1. Education   24%
2. Health   17%
3. Food   15%
4. Energy   14%
5. Art   12%
6. Science   5%
7. Environment   1%
8. Others   12%

Knowing the paltry amount of foundation money that gets directed at environmental organizations, one would have to wonder, why bother? There must be other, more fruitful ways of funding than to work (and I do mean *work*) for environmental grants, which are few and far between. There are some, and we will examine them at length in the chapters to follow, but one must remember the times we live in. As ongoing Republican administrations characteristically turn off the tap to charities and nonprofit organizations, they are left with nowhere to turn but to foundations.

There is flawed thinking on the part of foundations and grant seekers that the category "environment" is one dimensional, and within the confines of that one dimension, controversial. Foundation boards are populated by conservative people and a high percentage of environmentalists are, by nature, anything but conservative. Because these radicals are the most visible and frequently heard, the perception becomes that they represent the entire environmental movement.

This prompts an inherent distrust on both sides of the fence and if ever the twine shall twixt, it will be when both sides can see that environmentalism, by new findings and necessity, has changed and is now multi-faceted and more mainstream. In *Losing Ground: American Environmentalism at the Close of the Twentieth Century,* the aforementioned Mark Dowie suggests that if environmentalism can be viewed as more of an educational pursuit or as a champion for better health, then it can draw the attention of the foundations interested in these areas. If an environmental approach can lead to more efficient food production or energy generation, it would be viewed as a good thing.

From the glory days of the early seventies to the mundane present, the environmental movement has been complacent to stay in the corner it has painted itself into. However, the research and writing efforts, which seem to get better each year, suggest that like (surprise, surprise) the environment, the environmental movement is quite complex and ever-reaching into other fields of endeavor.

It's taken thirty-six years from the first Earth Day in 1970 for the most basic environmental issues to become ingrained in the national psyche. It can therefore be assumed that even the most conservative board members of any given foundation have at least a modicum of exposure to the issues that plague the environment. The trick is to somehow convince them that environmental issues are linked to the social issues that they care about. It's a strange paradox that while environmentalists bemoan the rigid thinking of foundation boards, they themselves spend relatively little effort in applying themselves to thinking outside-the-box. This outside-the-box thinking approach comes from realizing and truly believing that the environment exists at our fingertips just as much as it does at a national park in Montana. We are now faced with important environmental choices in every daily decision that we make. Environmentalists have to accept this fact before they can expect those that they criticize at every turn to accept it.

While only one percent of the current endowment pie

may seem like a pittance, it must be remembered that, by most middle class standards, it is a very large pie. Over two hundred grant makers, less than one-half of one percent of all grant makers, still fund up to 500 million dollars annually on environmental causes. The Environmental Grant Makers Association (EGA) annually publishes a roster of givers, and several other or related sources can be readily found on the Internet.

The grant business and the publishing business are remarkably alike. Similar to an author who annually purchases a copy of *Writers Market* because he/she wants to peddle their book to a publisher, a grant seeker must obtain and study lists of grant makers in a dogged attempt to *find the right fit*.

When a grant seeker pages through the EGA annual roster he must first determine if any given foundation has a track record of giving to foundations such as his. Do they have funds available for the next funding cycle? Do they give in his geographic area? Do they specify requirements for submitting a letter of interest, a request for funding, and a full-blown proposal? Do they publish an annual report? Do they have specific guidelines for grant submittals?

Upon zeroing in on a funder, a grant seeker should endeavor to learn as much as possible about them. He/she must be sure that they contact the right person, just as writers must be sure they get their manuscript into the hands of the right editor.

Private foundations usually want a short letter of interest whereby the grant seekers introduce their organizations and briefly (very briefly) describe their organization's purpose, goals, and/or mission statement. This could be one page long and rarely exceeds two. Corporations usually want a letter of intent, which is more detailed, running between three to five pages. Government agencies, as one would expect, want as much paper as you can send them; in other words, a full-blown proposal between twelve and twenty pages.

The typical full-blown grant request includes:

Cover Letter
Executive Summary
Needs Statement
Goals and Objectives
Methodology
Evaluation Process
Project Sustainability
Organization Background
Budget

With letters of interest and letters of intent, the grant seeker is more or less "fishing" for a funder to invite them to send in a more detailed proposal. A letter of interest describes the project and states specifically how much money is sought. A full-blown proposal has a mission statement, identifies personnel who will be working on the project, puts forth a timeline for completion, states the desired result, and (of course) clearly discloses the amount of money desired in the cover letter, in the mission statement, in the body of the text if applicable, and in the summary. Grant makers are suspicious of any proposal that doesn't clearly describe what the grant seeker's goals are and what amount is needed to achieve those goals.

Grant seekers are encouraged to follow any given foundation's proposal guidelines to the letter. This is not question regurgitation so typical of high school English tests, but rather a reflection of the fact that the seeker has followed every step, dotted every i, crossed every t. Reviewers within any given foundation are geared into their process, so seekers should not attempt to reinvent the wheel. It is of utmost importance to show respect for the foundation's efforts at outlining a process by following it step by step.

Timing can be everything. Investigate the grant's cycle. You must have your grant proposal in at the right time.

Grant Writing for Dummies by Bev Browning has excellent "cheat sheets" at the beginning of the book. Grant seekers need to have a clear understanding of their needs and be able to articulate those needs in their opening narrative. As the saying goes, "You will never get a second chance to make a good first impression," so clarity from the start is at a premium.

Grant seekers should imagine themselves signing up with a dating service. If you send out the wrong message as to who you are and what you need, your chances of finding a soul mate are greatly diminished. The chances are that you will go on many dates, spend a lot of money, and wind up truly miserable, while all the time hating the dating service for a situation that is entirely your own fault. Getting real with itself is the most important thing a grant seeking organization can do. It simply makes all the other steps easier.

Foundations are inundated with proposals from grant seekers, frequently wading through five thousand a year or funding cycle. With this kind of volume they have little choice but to think and act like book editors, who make extremely fast decisions based on the sender's apparent professionalism and the quality of writing. Employ strong, positive, active language and avoid "proposalese," which a seasoned reviewer can spot in a heartbeat. In this environment, the strength of the cover letter most often determines whether they will so much as read the first paragraph of the narrative or simply toss everything into the dreaded "slush pile" to be sorted through by junior editors (reviewers) to be responded to on an "as time allows" basis.

Just as in publishing, a quick response is bad news, a response at sixty to ninety days could possibly be good news, and no response is no news, or in reality, horrible news. Life is not fair. Sometimes those most deserving of a grant do not get it. Do not allow a failed request to become an excuse to quit trying.

Let's assume, for the moment, that your grant proposal is the one in five hundred that gets accepted for funding—what then? After a titanic celebration, dig your heels in, because this is when the work really begins. Up until say 1969 such a thing as "free money" existed in the foundation world. This is a thing of the past. Foundations now look upon nonprofits that they fund as partners. You will be expected to deliver on the promise outlined in your eloquently written proposal. In other words, you will be held *accountable*. In particular, foundation personnel will expect to see how their money was spent and whether or not there was any mismanagement on the part of the grant seeker. Reprisals on the part of foundations toward grant seekers who fail to perform are rare. In such cases, it is usually an eternity or longer before that particular grant seeker will ever see any money from that particular foundation again.

Remember the dating service analogy? If you disappoint her/him then he/she won't return your phone calls and if she says, "I'll get back to you," it means you will never see her again. For this reason, grant management is even more important than grant writing.

There's a saying in the consulting field that goes, "The best time to look for work is when you have work." Nothing could be truer in the grant acquisition business. The need for funding is eternal. Once an organization becomes dependent on grants it can never receive enough of them, which is to say the best time to write a grant proposal is immediately upon receiving a grant.

Management of grants allocated to environmental endeavors is quite different from a school grant, where you count the students and order the books. This can be especially true with projects such as habitat restoration, where the results are difficult to see and may take years to prove.

Remember that grant makers, to a fault, are conservative. This is why such a low percentage of available funding goes to environmental causes after all. Regrettably, accountability sometimes means stepping up to the plate and admitting that a project failed.

Invariably, environmental issues are more complex than social issues unless, of course, you can prove that they are one and the same. Invariably, failure will be part of the mix. Foundation personnel, despite their conservative nature, are people too. As with any other endeavor, the best way to work with people is to try to understand them. Failure is like crossing a line that can't be erased. In fact, it will be there forever, for everyone to see. If a grant seeker has been honest and open with a funder, then there will be a good chance that they will feel emotionally as well as financially invested in a project. In this climate a new line needs to be redrawn, perhaps with a better understanding of what results to realistically expect. The only time a failure can leave a lasting scar is when those who failed refuse to try again.

Chapter Two: Quotes
Fund Raising Strategies

What sets the Seven Faces framework apart from other systems is that it is donor-centered. It involves a detailed understanding of the concerns, interests, needs, and motivations of affluent individual donors as they think about philanthropy. By categorizing wealthy donors into seven motivational types, development officers and nonprofit executives gain new perspectives for understanding and cultivating their donor base. For example, Communitarians are defined as business owners motivated to improve the quality of life in their own communities and to reinforce their personal networks. They often become major donors to local, community-oriented nonprofits. Another group of donors, called Investors, has general interest in philanthropy but specific interest in managing their personal financial portfolios, (often assets derived from private business ownership) and in taking full advantage of the various tax and estate planning benefits of charitable contributions. Each of the other five Faces—Repayers, the Devout, Altruists, Dynasts, and Socialites—has its own distinctive profile.[5]

> *The Seven Faces of Philanthropy*
> Russ Alan Prince
> Karen Maru File

The enviable mystique that surrounds those who are successful at fund raising is nothing more, in my experience, than the attitude those individuals have about the process.

They know it is hard work, but it is worth it.

They are passionate about the causes for which they are raising money.

They come not as beggars, but as individuals offering others rare opportunities to invest in the future of their communities.

They are the catalysts for converting citizens to donor-investors in the organizations whose values they share.

They find the process to be satisfying and gratifying.

They see it as a way of involving people known and unknown to them in organizations that are making a difference in their communities.[6]

Beyond Fund Raising
Kay Sprinkle Grace

The several methods and techniques of fundraising are the tools used for (not the purpose of) fund development. The grand design for their use can be illustrated as a pyramid that has three levels of fundraising activity; (1) annual giving, (2) major giving, and (3) estate or planned giving (see Exhibit 1-2). Volunteers and donors are invited to begin their relationship by accepting information about the organization. Building the relationship will take time and will involve repeated opportunities for giving. In this way, their interest and personal involvement will increase to a level where investment decisions will be made. To spearhead the attainment of these levels of continuing relationships, the fund development department will be asked to play several roles. . . .

Fundraising is a "responsibility system," ethical at its base and tied to a larger complex of authority, control, and responsibility. Honesty, openness, and accountability are therefore essential to the integrity and credibility of fundraisers. The professional fundraiser is ethical and virtuous as well; wholehearted, persistent, and impartial. The purpose of fundraising is more than marketing, more than promotion, more than the money raised. Its value is in the results accomplished by the organization's use of the money. Fund development is the process where mission and purposes are matched with the public's desire to help; "people helping people" is carried out through fund development activities.[7]

Fundraising Fundamentals
James M. Greenfield

Chapter Two

Fund Raising Strategies

Imagine that you have just won the lottery. Financial security is no longer an issue in your life (or so you think). Now what do you do?

You would probably make up a list of family and friends that you would like to help out. A list so long, in fact, that to fulfill it would mean that you would go through all the lottery money before you spent any on yourself. So you cut the amount you planned to give everyone and, upon review, you cut it again. Then, sadly, you start cutting your list of family and friends based on whom you like best or on their needs. This having money and wanting to be generous with it is not as easy as it had seemed.

There are people out there who have won the lottery of life. Either through inheritance, hard work, good luck, or divine intervention that led to a windfall, they have far more money than the rest of us, and as far as the rest of us are concerned, far more money than they need. This is why I say that money turns people into animals. It prompts the most base behaviors of jealously, greed, resentment, contempt, vindictiveness, hatred, spite, and malice. Here's a contradicting thought to ponder. While money can be and often is the root of all evil, in the hands of the right person(s), it can be the catalyst of great good.

Three-quarters of all money given to charities and other causes is given as direct donations or bequests from private individuals. So, it can be said that money didn't turn these people into animals. Who are these people and why do they give? Russ Alan Prince and Karen Maru File have conducted exhaustive research to find out exactly this and have published their findings in *The Seven Faces of Philanthropy: A New Approach to Cultivating Major Donors,* which I will paraphrase below:

The Communitarian (26%), believes that charitable giving makes sense in that it promotes his own business by putting it in a good light. They usually give to well run charities that conduct themselves in a business-like manner.

The Devout (21%), believe that giving is God's will. They give almost exclusively to religious causes usually associated with the church they attend.

The Investor (15%), while he/she may have a philanthropic heart, is also a realist. They give to take advantage of tax breaks, which help strengthen the rest of their investment portfolio. They give mostly to umbrella organizations such as the United Way because they function on a theory similar to safe mutual funds, which spread risk across a number of businesses (charities).

The Socialite (11%), loves to give and make a party or event out of it. This ties into their outgoing hob-knobbing personalities.

The Altruist (9%), gives because it feels right. Rarely are they in it for the notoriety or the glory. They spurn the pat on the back and give primarily to social causes.

The Repayer (10%), feels a debt to society or an institution that has helped her/him up in their lives. They frequently give to colleges they attended and/or hospitals that have cured them.

The Dynast (8%), gives primarily because it's a family tradition and not to do so would be going against convention and tradition. Dynasts are unique in that they usually want to cut their own path in life. Although they follow their parents giving lifestyles they frequently choose their own pet charities other than the ones their parents give to.

The descriptions of these personality types and their motivations for giving are obviously streamlined. One individual may possess elements of two or more profiles. What's important to remember is that this type of profiling, as broad based as it is, does afford fund seekers a jumping off point. Just as we saw with grant giving and procurement, time is saved on both sides of the fence when one is able to *find the right fit*.

Organizations seeking funding leave no donor stone unturned. They know from what section of the population and what donor personality they can reasonably expect their best chance of success. These organizations are typically set up as nonprofits or not-for-profit entities. They are similar to foundations in that they receive favorable (or so it would seem) treatment from the Internal Revenue Service. While foundations typically are taxed at a rate of two percent, true nonprofits are indeed tax-exempt.

While nonprofits are set up like for-profit corporations or are, in fact, corporations, the comparison ends there. Nonprofits have a mission statement and are dedicated to a cause. Their boards are strictly comprised of unpaid volunteers. While their staff receives salaries, there is no flagrant overcompensation beyond that—no outrageous bonuses, no stock options, and no "golden parachutes" for retiring or fired executives. Corporations are dedicated to making money and that is a cause unto itself. It's an issue of who really benefits. The bulk of a nonprofit's income goes to the benefit of their stated cause. The law specifically states that income generated can pay salaries and overhead, but beyond that, it must be plowed like rotated crops back into the organization for the benefit of the people/causes it defines in its urgent mission statement. The most major difference between for-profit companies and nonprofits is that the latter is required to keep its books open for public review. I wonder if corporations would have a problem with this?

If a nonprofit dissolves, the money it has on its books must be given away to line the coffers of a similar organization. So, in theory and in practice, not-for-profit businesses are no more like slash and burn, seek and destroy, raid and pillage, to-hell-with-the-widows-and-orphans corporations than the man on the moon. This is good. They must, however, be managed in a business-like fashion and be just as accountable to their supporters as a corporation is to its board of directors and stockholders.

The income of a nonprofit that cannot be in the form of profit (hence the name nonprofit) still needs to be reported to and scrutinized by the world's most frightening and omnipotent government agency—the Internal Revenue Service, the IRS, the "feds." Since it is always they who have the last word, let's examine how the IRS defines a nonprofit business. Brace yourself, because we are about to embark on a dark and doleful journey into the murky newsprint world of IRS publications and forms—many forms.

The US Department of the Treasury "Publication 557:

Tax-Exempt Status for Your Organization" consists of sixty-three pages of the most confusing, unclear, frustrating and annoying verbiage you will ever encounter. In short, it is the type of pamphlet only a fifties-era accountant could love. Buy *Nonprofit Kit for Dummies* by Stan Hutton and Frances Phillips if you harbor any hope at all in navigating the convoluted treachery of "Publication 557." The "cheat sheets" are worth their weight in gold and the CD can be a tremendous help to getting an anticipated nonprofit business up and running.

Know that if you wish to establish a not-for-profit company the most important thing that you could possibly do is file the infamous 501(c) (3) forms (or one of its hybrids) with the IRS, wait three to six months for a determination as to your tax-exempt status, and pray fervently that it doesn't get sent back to you for further clarification(s). 501(c) (3) applies to the hopes and aspirations of literary presses, educational support groups, religious organizations, scientific institutes, and various charities.

What the IRS (and eventual contributors) really want to know is: is your business truly worthy of tax-exempt status? This, and whether or not you have a firm grasp on what a nonprofit truly is. In its most basic essence, the government allows nonprofits because society benefits. A contented society is one that only rarely requires reigning in.

Peace and tranquility are the oil on the cogs of the governmental machine. So, not-for-profits are smiled upon as the altruistic entities that are in place to provide the services that big government doesn't want to be bothered with. But just because it doesn't want to be bothered doesn't mean it's adverse to sticking its oar in often enough to make sure that it isn't getting ripped off. At the start up of the nonprofit paper chase, a

Federal Employee Identification Number (EIN) must be obtained in order to fill out form number 1023, which is the document that kicks off the establishment process of a 501 (c) (3) corporation (or any of its hybrids). The most important thing in 1023 will be your mission statement, which should be short, sweet, and to the point. Let's say that my wife wanted to start an environmental press with a name like, oh I don't know, perhaps like—Ribbonwood Press? The mission statement might say something such as this:

> *Ribbonwood Press is dedicated to championing environmental causes and promoting sustainable country living. Ribbonwood will help to launch the literary careers of new and innovative writers for the enlightenment of the public at large.*
>
> or
>
> *Ribbonwood Press is dedicated to the ideal of exposing new environmental writers to a larger audience, and promoting the virtues of country living.*
>
> or
>
> *Ribbonwood Press aids emerging authors in finding their readership, benefiting the environment, and country living.*

Most nonprofits that file their paperwork properly enough to appear legit are put on a five-year trial period, at the end of which the IRS will decide if they truly function as a not-for-profit entity or if they have crossed the line into functioning as a for-profit venture. There will be hell to pay if that line was crossed and penalties (the IRS can be *very* penal) levied against previous incorrectly reported income. The five-year trial period is, of course, a catch-22 invention of the IRS, as the agency wants three years of past tax returns from new organizations at the time of filing form 1023. These organizations are *new* and simply don't have them. By creating this five-year tax limbo, the IRS gives itself the best of both worlds. They can expend relatively little effort while they ignore you and leave the door wide open through which to easily pounce later. Let's assume, for the moment, that the 501 (c) (3) application is filled out properly and the IRS finds (for the time being) that the business is a legitimate nonprofit. Now the real work begins.

Operating budgets must be developed, job descriptions prepared, insurances drawn, state tax authorities notified, client lists initiated, a fund raising plan formulated, and a massive colossal party thrown.

The name of the business must be stated. The purpose of the business must be clear. Those who will benefit by the business must be identified. The IRS and the contributors need to know.

On IRS Form 1023 the board of directors must be listed. Since directors should not receive compensation it is best to keep anyone that's essential to the operation, yet in need of a paycheck, off the board and included instead as a member of key staff. This key staff will also be noted on Form 1023.

So now it's clear what the mission is, who this mission will help, and who will guide the nonprofit ship on its voyage.

The next day, while coping with the after effects of a rattling good hangover, you come to realize that the most important thing, in terms of keeping the business alive and healthy, will be the fund raising element. Remember the statement in the prelude: *Money that funds projects establishes a momentum all its own that is known as cash flow. Good cash flow can and often does hide a multitude of organizational and managerial sins.* Not that these sins can be ongoing. Inefficiencies will be spotted in a heartbeat by IRS personnel when they review annual form 990, five-and-a-half months from the business's opening date. A legitimately prepared 990 is what keeps nonprofits in the not-for-profit business.

Income is the lifeblood of any business and to keep a nonprofit afloat income must come from unerring and unending fund raising. The most important thing with fund raising is to have a target to shoot at. A realistic budget must be set so that everyone in the organization knows what they are working toward. If the staff doesn't believe in the budget or thinks it's unachievably high, there will be dissention in the ranks that will become a cancer to the group effort. As with time schedules, the object of budgets is to see that they're met. This is what professional businesses do, and contrary to popular belief, the vast majority of nonprofits are professionally run businesses.

With a budget set, a plan of attack must be developed. *Where will the funds come from?* A partial listing would include:

Private individuals.
Various types of foundations.
Memberships.
Events and benefits.

A list needs to be made up of every potential human being on the planet who might contemplate giving to the organization. People are inherently uncomfortable with asking friends and family for money, and in the not-for-profit world, they need to get over it. Remember that this is not a handout to benefit you. This is a credible organization with a just cause that needs funding. While the big mega-contributor gets a lot of the glory, smaller contributors usually outdistance their donated dollars. Any given small contribution seems like a drop in a bucket, but many drops will eventually fill a bucket. A small percentage of a lot sometimes comes to more than a large percentage of a few. All potential donors must be wooed. As the saying goes, "Edit your list and you edit your profits." *A nonprofit's donor list is its holy grail.* Most donors of large sums must be pampered to the point of hand holding and/or getting them publicity. This is especially true of business donors who use the good will to help promote their own businesses. If they act like they want illumination, put a glowing spotlight on them.

Foundations were discussed in chapter one and I'll refer you to it except to make note of the fact that some kinds of gifts cannot help you in the short term. Endowments are designed to live in perpetuity. The amount given can be invested in any number of interest bearing vehicles but the principal can't be touched. Only the interest, dividend, or other compensation above and beyond the original donated amount can be spent by the nonprofit. This news is not too terribly upsetting as anyone giving an endowment obviously feels that the organization is going to survive the test of time. Endowments should be viewed as a supreme vote of confidence.

Not every organization is structured to offer memberships and many that are don't bother to. This is short-sighted ignorance of a profit center that's capable of generating twenty percent of gross revenues. Members want to feel *invested* in an organization. The more informed they are, the more important they feel. While few nonprofits can afford to put out the glossy magazines of the "big three" (Audubon Society, Nature Conservancy, Sierra Club), bimonthly newsletters on newsprint, inexpensive quarterlies, or even regular updates posted on a web site are not out of the question. The more you invest in your membership the more they invest in you.

Events and benefits can be wildly successful or they can bury a nonprofit in debt. A rule of thumb well worth remembering is that even a wildly successful event or benefit costs at least half of the gross receipts it generates. If the attendance quota cannot be guaranteed then this fund raising strategy should be avoided like the plague.

Misconceptions about the "nonprofit sector" abound, especially among those that comprise "conventional" for-profit businesses. Here are some statistics to ponder:

Aggregate annual budgets of all nonprofits:	675 billion
Money released from budgets directly into nonprofit causes:	150 billion
Percentage of Gross Domestic Product (GDP):	8%
Unpaid volunteer workers:	92 million
Value of volunteers' hours:	200 billion
Annual donor contributions to nonprofits:	190 billion
Donor contributions going to nonprofit environmental causes:	3%

Similar to the abysmal performance of foundations toward supporting environmental nonprofits, other private sources of monetary support, including individual citizens, do not appear "invested" in environmental causes either. Clearly, environmentalism is not getting its market share, which is to say its fair share.

In light of this information it appears that we need even more environmental organizations especially at the local grassroots level. While it may seem like an insurmountable amount of work for pitiful little gained, environmentalists can't afford to give up. A small grassroots group can always lay the ground work to have a vehicle in place that can clear the way for a larger group, perhaps one of the "big three" or an entity such as the Trust for Public Land, to come in and mobilize quickly. Therefore, small grassroots efforts can be viewed as the guerilla fighters in the battle to save the environment.

Small nonprofit groups must continue and proliferate in the environmental movement. First, to help capture a larger market share of the not-for-profit sector's overall monetary pie. Secondly, they are often the only legally recognized entities that can ask for governmental and private contributions. Try doing this if you're a for-profit corporation.

So, guerilla fighters of the environmental movement, accept this challenge on your own turf. May the number of grassroots nonprofit environmental groups be like the stars in the sky. It may be the only way mankind will be able to continue looking at them.

Chapter Three: Quotes
Promoting Volunteerism

. . . *March 31, 1933, Congress gave the president the authority to proceed, at the same time empowering him to use any and all government departments that might be required. Initially involving about 250,000 men located in 1,330 camps, the Emergency Conservation Work Act (ECW), implemented by Presidential Executive Order No. 6101 on April 5, 1933, created the Civilian Conservation Corp. Especially aimed at the nation's forest lands, specific goals included "the prevention of forest fires, floods and soil erosion, plant pest and disease control, and the construction, maintenance or repair of paths, trails, and fire-lanes in the national parks and national forests, as well as similar work in state forest lands. Of course, with almost fourteen million unemployed in the United States by March 1933, the numbers enrolled were relatively small, but for those involved, the program provided a physical and spiritual lift of immeasurable value. . . .*

By any standard, the accomplishments of the CCC were impressive. Over 3,400,000 men had been enrolled by the time of its demise and their erosion control projects had benefited approximately forty million acres of farmland. In addition, among other things, 800 state parks were developed, 125,000 miles of roads were built. 814,000 acres of range land revegetated, between two and three billion trees planted, and over six million days were expended in fire fighting (in which 29 enrollees lost their lives). The total value of the CCC's work to the nation was estimated to be over two billion dollars, but its worth to the lives of the men that it touched, and the life of the citizenry as a whole, was incalculable.[8]

The CCC Chronicles
Alfred Emile Cornebise

Critics outside of the Peace Corps family circle largely target volunteers' motives and the agency's capability to effect lasting change. The stereotype of PCVs as hippie throwbacks with too much free time on their hands is sometimes embraced by these detractors. They not only pigeonhole the volunteer experience as yet another thrill for Gen Xers,

Mobilizing the Green Revolution

but wonder what contributions to third world development a twenty-two-year-old fine arts major can truly make. They point to the failures of relatively affluent development agencies such as the World Bank, the U.S. Agency for International Development (USAID), or the United Nations Development Program (UNDP) and wonder how, in comparison, a nickel-and-dime operation like the Peace Corps can combat issues of global importance. Lastly, critics insist that Peace Corps volunteers themselves are the prime beneficiaries of their service abroad. For PCVs, they argue, the experience is an opportunity to learn another language, see some of the world, and enrich their personal world view, all on the taxpayers' bill. For HCNs, they say, it provides a succession of random Americans intruding on their culture, living off of their generosity, and leaving once the novelty wears off.

As you consider joining, factor in the Peace Corps' criticisms, but keep in mind that the organization is generally praised for its persistence in educating and helping the world, one person at a time.[9]

So You Want to Join the Peace Corps?
Dillon Banejee

At warp-speed we are challenged to become part of societies' great transformation, not simply as "tag-alongs" or "spectators," but as part of the driving force of participants who envision a brighter tomorrow and are practical enough to understand that it must be built on a better today. . . .

The road to the future is as short as tomorrow and as long as "forever." It is more easily traveled when a good map is at hand, and I personally believe that good maps are formed by compiling solid information, clear directions and offering the signs that tell you what's ahead.[10]

Megatrends & Volunteerism
Sue Vineyard

34

Chapter Three

Promoting Volunteerism

Never volunteer. This has been an axiom of American culture since soldiers were conscripted into service during the Civil War in the early 1860s. With this negative declaration ingrained in our national psyche it seems miraculous that anyone does indeed volunteer for anything. But volunteer we do, and the country is better off for it.

In similar fashion to grants and fund raising there are those that have a need to give and those that need to be given to. What facilitates these desires is that each is able to find the other. Their chances are greatly enhanced when either or both acquire the innate ability to (once again) *find the right fit.*

Our abbreviated history of volunteerism starts in the 1930s. When the stock market crashed on October 29th, 1929, leading some of the immediately destitute to jump from high-rise office windows to their death, it concurrently led to the financial death of the nation. America, reeling from the aftermath of businesses being devalued overnight, was thrust into the Great Depression although anyone who lived through it will tell you that there was nothing great about it. Newly elected president Herbert Hoover had run on the same premise of preceding Republican president Calvin Coolidge's campaign promise of, "a chicken in every pot." This ominously foreshadowed events to come in a very hungry America that blamed its misfortune on him. Americans vented their wrath by referring to the Republican's chicken as a "Hoover Hog." They spitefully voted him out of office in 1932. In fairness to Hoover, if Jesus of Nazareth would have been the incumbent in '32 he would have lost the election by just as big a landslide.

Newly elected Democratic president Franklin Delano Roosevelt (FDR) was no stranger to hardship. He fell victim to polio at the unlikely age of thirty-nine and was to run the country from a wheelchair unbeknownst to the majority of the population in front of whom he always stood at public assemblies. Roosevelt strived to reunite the country by utilizing extended radio messages affectionately known to the public as "fireside chats." Roosevelt spoke of a plan, a "New Deal," and the country believed him. To understand why they believed him one has to study the context of history through a broader lens.

America had had its share of ups and downs during the first century-and-a-half of her existence. 1865 and the tumultuous years after the Civil War were exceedingly trying. Lincoln had somehow managed to keep the Union together, perhaps galvanized its resolve and bonded national compassion in death. We were a country that begrudgingly forgave each other. Forgave and moved on.

World War I was a shocker, producing mass death on a scale never before imaginable, and a realization that the world would never be the same. When our men came home they were scarred with the memory of being "over there."

Woodrow Wilson, our twenty-eighth president, had led the nation through the Great War that he openly opposed entering into. The most intellectual president since Madison and the only one to ever hold a doctorate, he understood that the nation could never again exist isolated from the world. He was the driving force behind the formation of the League of Nations, the precursor to the United Nations. The League was viewed as an organization that would prevent anything even remotely close to the First Great War from happening again. Wilson saw the need to smooth out the wide wave-like fluctuations of the American economy and created the Federal Reserve Bank and the Federal Trade Commission. America entered a period of posterity and was on automatic pilot when he voluntarily left office in 1921.

There didn't appear to be any way our government could screw this up. Enter Warren Gamaliel Harding, the nation's twenty-ninth president, with his "poker cabinet" and the Teapot Dome Scandal. Somebody was dealing from the bottom of the deck but not without consequences. Between extramarital affairs, illegitimate children, suicidal cabinet members, and selling the country's oil reserves to line his pockets, Harding was a busy guy. Next to him President Clinton looks like a choirboy. History remembers him as our worst president. He died in his office of a stroke on August 2nd, 1923, thus ending mounting support for impeachment proceedings.

Into the lurch stepped Vice President Calvin Coolidge, a man with an apparent charisma bypass operation. A man of few words, Coolidge's most quotable quote came when a woman told him, "You must talk to me, Mr. President. I made a bet today that I could get more than two words out of you." Coolidge responded, "You lose." The country was on automatic pilot. Why change horses in the middle of the stream? Coolidge was a passive bystander during his own 1924 presidential election campaign, not even bothering to deliver a speech until the last week. His supporters coined the phrase,

"Keep cool with Coolidge." There was, of course, that, "chicken in every pot" thing and the economy was strong, so why worry? In an uncharacteristic flatulence of wordiness Coolidge had said, "The business of America is business." The rearview mirror of history reveals that it's doubtful if he really believed it. In his typical terse fashion, he announced that, "I do not choose to run for president in 1928." He didn't explain why. Coolidge, ever an austere, conservative, and practical man, had seen the fiesta of paper wealth creation that was rampant at the time. The problem with being on automatic pilot is that everyone forgets to check the gas tank. Coolidge certainly saw the committing of economic sins and got out while the getting was good, leaving Hoover to hold the bag.

It's been said of Hoover that, "He took the heat of the Great Depression and did little to resolve it." Staunchly conservative to a fault, Hoover refused to step in and try to bail the country out. Some say he didn't fully understand the breadth of the problem until it was completely out of control. Stupid people are not elected president—sometimes insensitive people are—especially Republicans. Hoover himself was a fiscally responsible individual of Quaker faith. To his credit he refused the then $75,000 annual presidential salary. He wasn't personally affected by the depression, and completely out of touch with the common man, he failed to understand why others couldn't rise above it. Poor Hoover was history's casualty to poor timing and even poorer circumstances.

Prior to taking office on March 4th, 1929, Hoover was witness to five economic warning flares lighting up a sky that no one in America seemed to be looking at. The banking industry, even with Wilson's Federal Reserve, was in chaos. Six hundred institutions a year closed during Coolidge's term. Agriculture had been struggling since the dawn of the decade, a victim to its own glut of under-priced goods brought on by unchecked overproduction. With Theodore Roosevelt out of office, corporate injustices began to abound again and the target of their greed was their own employees. A lack of adequate salaries led to decreased buying power for goods and services. High tariffs, the love child of a renewed growing isolationist movement, discouraged international trade. And last, but certainly not least, was the extension of vast lines of credit to a populace who didn't know how to manage it. Stocks could be purchased on twenty-five percent margin, which lead to a paper feeding frenzy that drove the market up, up, up, like the Stratosphere in Las Vegas. But then there's that point when the seat stops and you get the sensation that you're being catapulted into space. It's a sensation of sheer terror and you're glad when the seatbelt catches you—until you start to plummet down.

And did America ever plummet down. First were the darling dandy recreated riverboat gambler "investors" who made the roaring twenties roar. They jumped from the high-rises to their deaths rather than face the embarrassment of calamitous instantaneous financial ruin. Then like lemmings falling over a cliff, the rest of the country followed. In less than a year's time four million Americans were out of work. Within three years, at the start of 1933, one in every four working-aged citizens didn't have a job, with little chance of getting one. In similar fashion to the job count, one in every four banks had likewise failed. From the fire to the frying pan, dust began blowing in from Oklahoma and marring the view of that financial blue sky in the east that no one bothered to notice. Families were set adrift. Responsible citizens, especially young men just coming of working age, became hobos overnight and rode the nation's rails, as chronicled by folk singer Woody

Guthrie. Displaced dustbowl farmers couldn't go east as their relatives couldn't afford to take them in, so they pushed west to California and onto the harrowing pages of John Steinbeck's *Grapes of Wrath*. Poor Hoover must have felt like the recipient of unending sniper fire. He couldn't determine where the shots were coming from. If ever there were an American president in the wrong place at the wrong time it was him. Poor Hoover, history refuses to forgive him the sins of Harding and Coolidge. Embittered, Hoover refused to forgive history, saying on the record, "Blessed are the young for they shall inherit the national debt."

After twelve years of Republican mismanagement and tomfoolery the country was willing to listen to anyone, even that brash young governor of New York with his wild newfangled ideas and his talk of a "New Deal." Franklin Delano Roosevelt stepped onto the world stage.

The country was rudderless and fed up. The people felt the Republicans had been dealing from the bottom of the deck for over a decade. The party was in deep, deep doodoo and no one stood a chance of winning the 1932 election so they offered up poor Hoover as their sacrificial lamb. Dukakis and Perot could have beaten him in this climate of distrust and disgust boarding on hatred. Hoover was marched off to the slaughterhouse masquerading as the nation's electoral college, losing by a margin of 472 to 59, which was the worst defeat in history. Americans shed few tears for poor Hoover. As with most massacres the thirst for blood dulled their senses and when they regained them they had to ask themselves, "Just what the hell is this New Deal all about?"

The New Deal was about creating opportunity. About jumpstarting the stalled American economy. About instilling hope in a land that had lost all hope. It wasn't nearly as well-thought-out or well-managed as some historians would like to have us believe. What it did do was create human motivation and motivation can move mountains.

The platform of the New Deal was built upon programs that would create jobs. Nothing restores lost self-respect like work, especially work that enables you to pay your own way.

In the course of two years Roosevelt birthed the Civilian Conservation Corps (CCC), the Tennessee Valley Authority (TVA), the Works Progress Administration (WPA), and the Rural Electrification Administration (REA). These were all jobs-based programs with tangible goods and/or benefits realized from the labor. In addition, he overhauled agriculture with the Agricultural Adjustment Act (AAA), which reduced crop surpluses. Then came the National Industrial Recovery Act, which promulgated 750 codes of fair competition to over five hundred types of businesses employing in excess of 20 million workers. The National Housing Act was instituted to aid the moribund housing industry. It birthed the Federal National Mortgage Association and the Federal Savings and Loan Insurance Corporation. Next came the Security and Exchange Commission (SEC), which regulated the stock market and choked out abuses.

Considering the sloth-like speed at which government moves, it's evident that Roosevelt was as busy as a one-legged man in an ass kicking contest. A modern day Robin Hood, he was hated by the rich and loved by the poor who, in similar fashion to utilizing the acronyms of his programs, took to calling him FDR. Critics say that his programs were only marginally successful, and that what really bailed the economy out was the onslaught of World War II, and the nation being dragged into it. There's no economy like a wartime economy.

Roosevelt's Civilian Conservation Corps (CCC) was set

up to build roads, plant trees, provide flood control, and initiate a myriad of other conservation projects, many within the confines of our national and state park systems. Run like a quasi-military operation, members did indeed wear surplus World War I uniforms and utilize tents and other equipment from that era. Retired officers were employed as directors. Young men volunteered and were given minimum pay of a dollar a day in addition to meals and housing, mostly in tent cities. The real value they would receive would be in on-the-job training.

The CCC touched the lives of over three million men in its nine-year life. Two hundred and fifty thousand joined after its inception in 1933. Five hundred thousand were in the Corps in 1935 during its watershed year. Was it successful? One of the instructors in one of the camps sent FDR this personal letter dated October 16th, 1937:

> *Dear Mr. Roosevelt:*
>
> *I take this means to extend to you my appreciation of your speech the other night. I assure you it gives me a feeling of the greatest security to know that we have a President that has the foresight and wisdom that you have shown.*
>
> *Please understand that I am an ex-service man and in a CCC camp drawing thirty six dollars per month and that before I came here have worked for three bushels of turnips per day boarding myself. Might I add that I am the father of six children, three of which are in high school. Of course I am not satisfied with the condition we are forced to live in because of the depression. Having been fortunate enough to have been with a firm for some eleven years previous to 1932 my family was used to the average standard of living, (1800. Annually). This is mentioned that you might know the drop in our living condition.*
>
> *If we were to be faced with the continued circumstances we*

find ourselves in, life would be hopeless indeed BUT what cheers us is the thought, not of the petty errors of petty politics, but the splendid vision you have and the progress you have made. It is very easy to visualize what would have happened these past years when at the time you took over the ship of state the waves of despair was washing over the whole country, had we not some one with courage enough to do the things you have done.

Your speech encourages us to "saw wood" and pull for the future you so courageously plan. It seems very dark indeed to us at times and personally I would like to hear you broadcast more often. It brings us out of the "Blues."

May our God watch over your every move and word and be with the leaders of our Nation.

Very respectfully,
Lawton L. Brown
Miller, Missouri

Wildly successful, I'd say.

The Civilization Conservation Corps was called "the tree army," and, true to that name, planted at least *two billion* trees. This is amply portrayed in Stanley Cohen's *The Tree Army: A Pictorial History of the Civilian Conservation Corps, 1933–1942*. With carbon dioxide-sucking trees being the number one deterrent to global warming and the "greenhouse effect," wouldn't it seem logical to start planting them by the billions again?

Owing to the times, the CCC camps were segregated. Most of the all-black camps were located in California. Olen Cole, Jr. provides an excellent account of the black experience in the CCC in *The African American Experience in the Civilian Conservation Corps*. Cole concedes that while the discrimination was definitely wrong the experience was right.

Another well-documented account of one of FDR's most

successful "alphabet agencies" is John A. Salmond's *The Civilian Conservation Corps 1933–1942: A New Deal Case Study* published in 1967.

Nearly every camp had a newspaper, which is well documented in Alfred Emile Cornebise's *The CCC Chronicles: Camp Newspapers of the Civilian Conservation Corps, 1933–1942.*

All but one title I researched had the same sickening dates tacked on: 1933–1942. It's the finality of those numbers that gets to me. I feel as if I'm reading someone's obituary while the green revolution is about infusing new life into environmental causes.

Aside from the 250,000 plus American deaths that occurred during the war to end all wars (to date) there was another untimely death that left a void in America. The CCC was abolished in 1942 in response to a need for able-bodied fighting men, which those in its ranks were.

The Civilian Conservation Corps (CCC) has now been defunct for sixty-five years. With the myriad of environmental calamities facing America there is only one thing left to do. Bring back Jack! And not a minute too soon.

The reasons this can't be done will most likely far outdistance the reasons why it can, for America has become a nation of pessimists and our politicians are living up to our low expectations. As a nation we have to expect more from our leaders in government. The CCC was successful because the conditions of the times created an air of desperation that caused young people to be receptive to something, anything, that might facilitate change in their lives. We are rapidly approaching the conditions of those times again.

The reason why I have waded through this unsolicited history lesson while dragging you along, dear reader, is to illustrate a fundamental point. Great presidents come along maybe once in a lifetime if we're lucky. I was born in 1951, a product of the "baby boom" if there ever was one. When I enter into conversations or interviews with members of my generation one of my favorite questions to ask someone is, "Name your top five presidents." I get a wide range of answers and with the sporadic exception of Kennedy none of them include a president more current than FDR. For the record I vote Lincoln, TR, FDR, Jefferson, and Madison. I believed in Kennedy because my parents believed in Kennedy but once I got older and started thinking for myself he dropped off my list. William Manchester's *One Brief Shining Moment* was just that—one moment, and not all that shining in retrospect. There are some eerie comparisons between Lincoln and Kennedy including the "twenty year curse" but the similarities end at trivia questions and don't translate to performance. Oh, I've seen more than enough poor presidents and one extremely bad one. Nixon, upon entering office, immediately doubled the presidential (his) salary to $200,000, and we all know where he went from there.

With the possible exception of Harry S. Truman, who I obviously was too young to remember, I can say with certainty that there has not yet been one great president in my lifetime. The point being? After fifty-five years I have accepted the fact that *I may never live to see one.*

The central issue of my life is environmentalism and I believe the century 2000 to 2100 will be marked by it. What the presidents Roosevelt did for nature in America was truly remarkable especially in light of the attitudes that persisted with the citizenry during their respective terms in office. I don't see anyone even remotely resembling the Roosevelts on the political horizon and I sincerely doubt that an American president will ever win the Nobel Peace Prize again. The point being? If it's going to be, it's up to me. We can't look to leadership as high as the president of our land because it doesn't exist. If environmentalists want to bring back the CCC they are going to have to do it themselves.

California and Wisconsin are trying, with Wisconsin even being forward thinking enough to have co-educational camps. These are token efforts in that the environmental problem is a national problem and efforts to bring the CCC back should occur on the national level. It's essentially a volunteer effort because, historically speaking, original camp populations were just happy to be off the streets and off the rails while doing something productive with their lives. The dollar-a-day pay was a confidence booster and usually got sent home to families. Today, even with the ravages of inflation, ten to twenty dollars a day would suffice. What's important to the success of any new CCC enrollees is the same thing that's important to the success of committed college students, that being that *they want to learn.* They must have an insatiable thirst for any knowledge that might improve the circumstances of their life. Even I would be willing to teach in a classroom like that. I used to unfairly say, "Those that can't do teach," until I grew up and realized that someone must have taught me something. Promoting volunteerism, I'm now prepared to pass it on down the line.

The Peace Corps, which were founded in March of 1961, is something John Fitzgerald Kennedy did do right. The goal of the program initially was and still is to promote better understanding between Americans and citizens of other countries. Volunteers are usually teachers or individuals with technical skills primarily in medicine and in food production. Anyone who is a citizen of the U.S. and over the age of eighteen can join up. Volunteers are compensated for living expenses only. It takes an admirable human being to be a Peace Corps volunteer and the tasks live up to their motto, "The toughest job you'll ever love." Eighty-five thousand volunteers passed through the program during its first twenty years. Today there are about six thousand Peace Corps volunteers spread about the globe on a yearly basis.

Lyndon Baynes Johnson, not one ever to be outdone by his predecessor Kennedy, founded the Job Corps in 1964 as an adjunct to his War on Poverty Program because poverty shouldn't exist in the "Great Society." Johnson at least had dreams, most of which were stifled by the ongoing war in South Viet Nam. The Job Corps provided training in residence to inner city primarily disadvantaged youth between the ages of sixteen and twenty-one. Arms of the program still exist today although all could use an uplifting economic shot in the arm. Johnson also promoted Volunteers in Service to America (VISTA), which acted as a domestic Peace Corps, infiltrating the ghettos of the nation to teach and work. Johnson at least had dreams. Where have they gone? His programs faded from the national scene just as he did. Leaving office on January 20th, 1969, he was the last American president to talk of such nonsense as a "Great Society." It's as if Americans don't believe in the compassion of Americans anymore. Or are we all looking in a mirror?

There's a sickening parallel between the dwindling American environment and the fading American volunteer effort. From European contact to today there is approximately two percent of pristine wilderness left. If you divide the nine years of the CCC's existence into its three million enrollees, you get 333,333 members per year. Then if you divide the first twenty years of the Peace Corps existence into its 85,000 members you get 4,250 persons per year. And what percentage of 333,333 is 4,250? *Two percent!* The parallel is that if the survival of the environment is now dependent on the breadth of the volunteer effort then we must strive to keep them both alive. Less human effort mean less habitat. More human effort can equate to more saved ground. It doesn't take a rocket scientist to know why Mark Dowie's book on the state of environmentalism in the US was aptly titled *Losing Ground.* There's nothing to it but to do it. If it's going to be, it's up to me.

The face staring back at me in the mirror is tired and drawn and wants to give up. A landscape architect should be able to make an impact in the environmental movement. I've devoted my entire career to nature, right? What a joke. I'm a clerk in a candy store trying to get rich kids to make up their mind so that the rest of the line can move. I deal with millionaires on a daily basis who routinely balk at my fee and ask, "Can't you do any better for me?"

What can you do for me? If it's not my clients it's my kids. And if it's not my kids it's somebody else's kids. Everybody wants something for nothing. It's the American way. Casinos abound built on flawed dreams of incomprehensible wealth lying just around the corner at the mere touch of a button. America has become the land of the big hit. Everyone has an equal chance to win the lottery just like in Orwell's *1984.*

My career as a landscape architect has become a grinding, numbing nightmare. If it's not the clients, it's the design review committees, experts at creating problems only they can solve. They beat me about the head and face with their inane comments. "This wall is too high. These colors don't match. The proportion is all wrong. This plant isn't on our list. I can't explain why, but this bothers me." On and on and on. This unrelenting cavalcade of bullshit. Jesus, how they bitch and whine about much to do about nothing. And God how I hate it.

I got a panicked call the other day. A developer's landscape architect had just thrown up his hands and quit. Could I, as a favor to them, go out to a local country club and get this issue resolved? *This was an emergency!* The problem? A wall adjacent to a fire lane that members of an exclusive country club occasionally rode their golf carts on to get to each others' parties, where they would trade mistresses, and diamonds, and BMWs, was just too high. This was an outrage and if something wasn't done about it immediately litigation was sure to ensue. I called in a marker with a member of the club's omnipotent design review committee and set out to play Solomon so as to mitigate this perversion to the human spirit and sensibilities.

As it turned out, the outlaw villain wall could only be seen if you went looking for it. It could easily be screened with a hedgerow of shrubs or softened with vines. It was going to take more than that, the design review board member told me. "Tear it down. Stagger the heights. You better come up with something. This situation is entirely unacceptable. This developer has gotten away with things before and we aren't going to stand for it anymore. Why just last year . . ." His voice became like the menacing drone of a swarm of blood thirsty mosquitoes, and all I could think of was getting away from him and this monumental "problem."

Dear Lord, is this what my life has become? Referee in a contest of affluent egos? Is this what I signed on for when I graduated college back in '74? I thought my classmates and I were going to change the world. Pawn on a rich man's chessboard. John C. Krieg, Landscape Architect and stroker of ruffled privileged silver-spooned feathers.

49

I'd conduct such important, life changing work down in the desert until late in the evenings. Then I'd go back up the hill to my house in Anza at four thousand feet in elevation on the high desert plateau. I'd travel in my beat up rough running pick-up truck kept company by the warm amber glow of the "check engine" light. I'd keep a watchful eye out and a keen nose open for forest fires in the surrounding hills because every spring, summer, and fall they're expected, like my uncle Vern would say, "Sure as shit." And every spring, summer, and fall rarely am I disappointed as the west is on fire due to careless thoughtless asinine cigarette smokers throwing their butts out into the waiting tinderbox brought about by even more asinine US Forest Service management practices. We are in the midst of the worst drought on record or off record if you talk to some of the Cahuilla who have lived here since time immemorial. You know, there just might be something to all this global warming noise.

When I descend what was once the "nigger Jim trail" into Anza (more coming on this in Ravings) my mind will turn to real estate developers who want to chop, slice, and dice her up and spit her out their blender in the image of their profit laden dreams. Maybe I should, maybe I could do something about it. And maybe not. I'm just too busy to get heavily involved. I'll write an article in the local paper now and then but that's about the extent of it. I'll be dead before it gets really bad, or so I hope. Tomorrow I'll descend back down to the desert, which is something akin to going to hell, ignoring these environmental problems (why not *emergencies?*) that engulf southern California. I'll be chasing that elusive pot of gold that lies at the end of a design review committee's letter of approval. John C. Krieg, Landscape Architect and arbitrator of arcane agendas.

Oh how I want to pack it in and leave it all behind me in

a wake of seething revulsion and hatred. Maybe I can help the environment by writing books about it, I tell myself. Maybe, but it's a slippery slope. The week before *Environmental Cognizance* came out I would lie awake at night staring at the ceiling. Instead of sheep I would count reviews scrolling before my shocked, disbelieving eyes:

A meaningless tomb spawned from the depraved mind of a deeply crazed and deranged crackpot who should be jailed and muzzled before he inflicts any more damage.

Carolyn Jong
Freudian Psychologists Monthly

The utterly confused and moronic ramblings of an idiot who will do more harm than good to the environment.

Niel Nonbeliever
Atheist Scientists Union

A spottily researched and totally pollyannic look at important issues. Call Krieg's take on the state of the planet environmentalism lite.

Jesus Garcia
Christian Biology Quarterly

There is no difference between buying this book and burning money.

Myron Mega-Bucks
Center For Freemillons

The deserts and chaparral's of the southwest have found their new Darth Vader.

Sibil Drivel
Comic Book Weekly

Worse yet, perhaps it wouldn't get reviewed at all. Maybe, in a fit of misguided compassion, critics would toss it in the trash can. So I'll write more books. Books on top of books. Books to the left, books to the right, stand up, sit down, fight, fight, fight. It's time to stop writing and start doing. Books might increase awareness but they won't save the environment. If it's going to be, it's up to me. It's time to take action. It's time for me to volunteer to do anything that will truly help.

I've just gotten back from a vacation/family reunion at the New Jersey shore. While there I walked two miles daily on the beach, which was exhilarating because it's been a long time since I have walked anywhere. Waves crashing, seagulls screeching. A misty morning marine fog so thick you felt the effort you were exerting to split it. The sloughs and oxbows of the inland rivers seemed to be in good health. The estuaries looked none the worse for wear. The shoreline of the Atlantic Ocean, the ground upon which my feet were falling, however, was littered with an inordinate number of shells. More shells, in fact, than I had ever noticed on any of my previous visits. When I brought this up in casual conversation it was dismissed as, "Some kind of die off, I guess." Jersey has the most nuclear power plants and active landfills in the United States and its just the forty-sixth largest state up there in the northeast nestled among all those other "little states." It's quality not quantity that matters, my New Jersean relatives tell me. But sometimes quantity tells you something. Like New Jersey's disproportionate number of nuclear plants and landfills in comparison to the number of shells strewing the shoreline. Maybe there's a link, "Some kind of die off, I guess?" I'd have to say you have probably guessed right. Any idea as to why the volunteerism rate in America is down to two percent of what it used to be? Care to hazard a guess as to why the environment is losing ground daily? What could it be? Some kind of die off, I guess.

My niece, twenty-seven and with an impending Ph.D. in law, plans to be a social crusader for children who can't speak for themselves and are caught up in a system that pushes them around until they are backed quietly into a corner from which they can be totally ignored. God bless her heart. She's not shy about voicing her take on America. "There's plenty of money to fix our problems, it's just that our government spends money on stupid things." I can't begin to tell you how proud I am of her, my niece the social malcontent and rabble rousing rebel in the making. When I look at young people she is certainly the exception rather than the rule. She's the one in ten thousand.

The vacation was too short and I got indoctrinated back into the hustling and bustling hell that would be my life at the start of the workweek as I shuffled through the Philadelphia Airport terminal after being frisked with detection machinery and eyed with the contempt usually reserved for common criminals. Long lines were stacked up behind the signs of those joined fast food joints with everyone pushing against each other for their daily quota of growth hormones and grease. It was daunting enough to force me to buy a sandwich from Wolfgang Puck for twelve dollars. At least it came in a snazzy, look at me, I-can-afford-to-throw-money away bag.

The three hour layover in Las Vegas was spent trying to read some research material while being interrupted by ring-ing, singing, chiming, beeping, blaring, buzzing, musical cell phones and the ensuing too loud and show-offish, listen to me, I-have-an-active-social-life conversations. Packing like canned sardines into our seats, I got sandwiched between a good looking, athletic young black man in a UNLV basketball uniform (he could have very well been a member of the team), and an attractive, well-conditioned teenage girl whose glittering t-shirt displayed "Goddess."

The plane lifted up over Las Vegas, a titanic-like, water sucking, desert gobbling monument to stupidity and greed. Soon, very soon—2020 soon—she will run headlong into her iceberg. Good, riddance say I. The plane winged out over the sere Mohave Desert, becoming more desertic by the minute. I read on and scribbled research notes only my wife Nancy can decipher onto a pad. They were talking across me as if I were a wall without a peephole. I caught snitches and snits of their conversation interspersed every other sentence with an affirmative "dude" or "tight." Maybe they were "hooking up" and the fossilized dinosaur sitting between them just couldn't comprehend how romantic sparks flew in the new millennium. I don't know.

The climatic event of this sojourn was when I spied Big Bear Lake, the glimmering jewel of the Mount San Gorgonio wilderness. I waited in silence, wondering if they would notice. To my amazement she did, exclaiming, "Big Bear! I love snowboarding!" "What else can you do?" he asked. "Water skiing, four-wheeling, clubbing," she answered, apparently pleased that this potpourri of activities spelled the dawn of a new teenaged utopia. This pleased him also, and I could only imagine that if they did "hook up" they might motor out to this lake in a nine-mile-per-gallon Hummer for a lively first date. Their concept of nature was that of something to be

54

shushed over or trampled upon, while afterward celebrating these conquests with a chilly libation.

Hadn't they noticed all the dead evergreen trees in the once verdant forest? Victims of severe drought, which so weakened them that they became prime targets for growing infestations of pine bark beetles. Didn't they see that the lake's water line was the lowest it had ever been? Were they conscience of the fact that there weren't any big bears left in California, the last Grizzly being shot in Fresno County in 1922? California's only remaining Grizzly is on the state flag. Beyond that, even if they did notice, would they care? These two did not appear to be likely candidates to volunteer to lend their time and sweat to an environmental cause any time soon.

Like most kids today they were not bad kids, they were just oblivious. I thought of our girls. They regularly pass through the office, which contains my most prized possession, a lumbering bookcase filled to the gills with just about every environmental title post-1995. You think I know this stuff because I'm smart? I've turned plagiarism into an art form. The girls would no more crack open one of these books than they would crack a nail doing dishes or taking out garbage. I tell them repeatedly that, "Reading is the key to knowledge. If you don't know something and can't afford to go to school, how will you learn?" They couldn't care less. They merely want to be successful, which in their viewpoint, more precisely means to be wealthy. They think that success will come looking for them and all they have to do is be receptive to the idea of it. Oblivious. The oldest is half-a-decade from thirty and already there's a bankruptcy of spirit. I don't think the environment can count on any volunteers among the three of them.

I suspect the kids on the plane did hook up. They left the

Ontario terminal together. She with the expensive skateboard under her arm, which she openly worried that someone working in baggage might steal. "You can't trust anyone these days. Now I wish I would have stowed it on board." He, furiously stabbing the buttons on his cell phone as if he were sending out an SOS to a flotilla of ships. They were probably heading inland toward LA, Joni Mitchell's city of the "fallen angels."[b] They would be greeted by smog, traffic congestion, power malls, and cracker box houses all in a row but they probably wouldn't even notice. Young love—isn't it grand?

I was headed back to Anza and these young people I worry so much about. I see them growing up in a world of diminishing economic opportunity and dwindling natural resources so sadly yet marvelously depicted in T.C. Boyle's *A Friend of the Earth*. We could very well be headed into the next Great Depression. I fret over young people across America. Eleanor Roosevelt, America's queen of compassion and wife of FDR, agonized also way back in 1934 when she wrote:

> *I have moments of real terror when I think we may be losing this generation. We have got to bring these young people into the active life of the community and make them feel they are necessary.*

It seems like only yesterday when I was an eager and willing recipient of the fruitful harvest of the golden age of rock and roll. The Who was singing a loud and raucous "Talking Bout My Generation," and now my generation is running the country. Of course, the generation we birthed, the too few that are paying attention anyways, accuse us of running it into the ground. They have a point, as most righteously indignant young people do. They remind me of a young person I knew when I was young. Now his face is tired and drawn and wants to give up as it stares back at me in the mirror. I can't give up, I won't give up, because I know what's at stake. I do, however, have a bone to pick with the majority of the generation my generation birthed who aren't paying attention. What the hell is wrong with you? Beyond that, look at the generation you are birthing. Is it we that have failed you? Or have you failed us? Are you aware that we are jointly failing our children and grandchildren? You are letting education take a backseat in America. You are letting corporations rape the land. You are accepting ineffective government by not turning out to vote. Do you really think government has your best interests at heart? "My, my, my, said a spider to a fly."ᶜ (Stones '65).

I can rage at them all I want and it's just a waste of time and energy. The only life I can control is my own. If it's going to be, it's up to me. It's time to get up off my posterior and try to become the person I thought I could be back in '74. The need for survival knocked the holy crap out of my ideals. For the last thirty years I've lacked the volition I thought I had back then. *What the hell is wrong with me?* For too many years I've existed within the comfortable confines of my own little environmental chapel. For too many years I've been preaching the green message to the choir.

It's time to stop saying, "Do as I say, don't do as I do." It's time to get up off my ass and do something. The best form of leadership, after all, comes from example. So now I finally see that I need to provide the answer to my own question. When the need is readily apparent and the cause environmentally just, what should *I* do?

Always volunteer.

57

Chapter Four: Quotes
Conscription of Manpower

I'm convinced that America itself, like so many of the people I write about, is in serious trouble. The essays in this book offer a glimpse of a society that has stopped chasing the fundamental tenets of its mythic dream. The nation has grown largely indifferent to abuses of power and social injustice. Flag-waving politicians still give lip service to the great American ideals of freedom, justice, equality, and opportunity, but in an era of preventive war and so-called conservative values, we've all but stopped pursuing them. And that's dangerous. Throughout our history the pursuit of those ideals—however imperfect the effort, however strained, timid, slow, and haphazard—was the only thing that made the United States special. . . .

Now where are we? At some point late in that postwar run, we took a wrong turn. That can-do era sputtered to an end, and we let the selfish, the vain, the greedy, and the incompetent take control of our nation and tell us what we can't do. We can't build first-class schools. We can't provide a reasonable wage for all working men and women. We can't follow through on the promise of Social Security. We can't deliver affordable drugs to the sick and infirm. We can't clean up the slums, or rescue the millions of children trapped in the clutches of poverty. We can't protect the environment. . . .[11]

Promises Betrayed: Waking Up from the American Dream
Bob Herbert

Since their invention, AMOs (administered mass organizations) have served regimes of rightist and leftist ideologies, they have appeared in countries with different political cultures and levels of economic development, and they have served purposes other than war. Indeed, many statesmen who have launched AMOs since 1945 have been unaware of their war-related origins. But whenever the AMO has operated, it has never completely lost its character as the civilian version of the conscript army. In many respects, the imprint of the three seed countries, which launched AMOs in a conscious endeavor to militarize civil society, has proved indelible. Granted that no two conscription societies have been exactly alike, the spread of the same basic type of institution to so many diverse settings underscores the derivative character of contemporary politics in most countries.[12]

The Conscription Society
George J. Kasza

Like many other contemporary criminologists, I continue to be an advocate of rehabilitation and social reintegration as correctional goals, in spite of the discouraging evidence noted above. In my opinion, a single-minded stress on punitive sanctions and state operated terror and intimidation to coerce citizens into law-abiding conduct is unworthy of a democratic society. On this point, many of the spokespersons for renewed emphasis upon punishment seem most willing to have severe penalties visited upon garden-variety lawbreakers. Surely it is ironic that these harsh recommendations are targeted upon population groups who are most vulnerable to the criminogenic influences of economic precariousness and other rents, tears, and imperfections in the social order. And there is abundant evidence at hand which indicates that it has been these same relatively powerless groups in our society who have received the most severe dispositions from the juvenile and criminal justice systems in the past.[13]

Changing the Lawbreaker
Don C. Gibson

Offending in adolescents peaks at around the age of 16–17 years (Wolfgand et al., 1987), accounted for by a rise in the number of offences committed by new offenders. There is also a relationship between juvenile and adult crime, with those individuals who receive convictions at an early age (10–12 years) being most likely to continue offending into adulthood.[14]

Making Sense with Offenders
Julia Houston

Chapter Four

Conscription of Manpower

It's on the news all too often. It's the subject of sensationalistic reporting and a vehicle by which the unscrupulous New Right coerces and intimidates votes from people who should know better if only they made the effort to be better informed. It's a problem to be sure and it's fast approaching epidemic proportions. An even bigger problem is the breadth of problems that created the problem in the first place and these are growing with each passing day.

It's an often heard social lament that goes like this: America's prison system is in shambles. It's too small, too poorly run, and doesn't accomplish any meaningful rehabilitation. Juvenile detention systems are worse and are little more than proving grounds for graduation to the "big house."

And then there's the situation in our schools, which are frequently so bad that teachers fear for their lives. From such institutions the hard cases either gravitate to the juvenile detention facilities or get kicked out on purpose or simply refuse to attend so that they can get on that free ride to nowhere known as "home schooling."

It's a, "damned if you do, damned if you don't" scenario. The financial costs of our criminal detention systems are staggering, and proponents argue that if they didn't exist the costs of the damage the detainees could inflict upon society, if allowed to run free, would be astronomical. Even more bad news and foreboding awaits in the future as the soon-to-be-realized social costs of the home schooling craze will be visited upon the nation a decade hence.

Has America gone mad? Why do we allow such a correctional system, which is nothing more than a whirlpool of social destruction? And what, if anything, can we do about it? The remedy must be a two-pronged approach. First, to try to improve on what is. Second, to remove the conditions that fanned the flames that allowed things to get to this point.

There are so many people arrested and subsequently convicted after a lengthy and costly (to the public) trial process that we don't have the space in our existing jails and prisons to house them all. House arrest has come to the forefront and I contend that, although not as good a training ground as prison for increasing more sophisticated criminal behavior, it is the incubator for developing new thought toward a career in crime.

Consider the merits of house arrest. The convict is detained in the exact environment from whence sprang the desperation for him to commit a criminal act in the first place. What would be different that would lead him to change? He is now given ample time and opportunity to figure out a methodology for committing home-based crime. Thus, it can be said that house arrest is birthing a new criminal cottage industry.

The concept of restitution has long been one of the main desires of the criminal justice system. Those that have had criminal acts levied against them are, in theory, supposed to be repaid. How does a criminal go about doing this even if he/she wanted to when the fruits of their labor while incarcerated don't even offset the costs of housing, feeding, and clothing them? Individualized restitution is an implausible fantasy and the concept should be abandoned in favor of one that might work. Perhaps the aggrieved could be given a choice of programs to which he/she could direct the efforts of their tormentors. While one step removed from an outright charitable contribution, at least something the victim cares about would receive some benefit. Restitution efforts should be directed toward those things that were wronged and/or harmed in the first place. Take the environment as an example.

Those that harm the environment should be punished in a manner that pays retribution to the environment. When my driver's license was suspended during my mid-life crisis, I was required to attend twenty hours of intensified driver's training where I was not only berated as being the scourge of the highways, but also shown the negative impacts of my behavior on my life and potentially on the lives of others. *I did learn something* that affected my future behavior. Poachers, the most despicable form of human life on the planet, should be taken out to the areas where the illegally slain game was killed and be forced to engage in habitat restoration for the benefit of that exact species.

The environment can, in fact, be employed to mitigate crime. Nature has a way of softening the hardest of mankind. The May–June 2005 edition of *Audubon* magazine ran an article by Maria Finn Dominguez entitled *2nd Chances: A Novel Prison Program in New York City Uses Nature to Teach Inmates About Life's Larger Lessons.*

The article is about Rikers Island Prison outside of New York, which holds approximately twelve thousand detainees awaiting trial who are unable to post bail and about four thousand prisoners with sentences of one year or less. Not quite the hard core, but certainly on the verge of becoming hard core.

James Jiler of the New York Horticultural Society has overseen a gardening program for the last three years. Three hundred students have utilized the program to combat oppressive boredom and as a vehicle to get their lives back on track. On only two acres of ground they have established a vegetable garden productive enough to stock homeless shelters in the most destitute parts of Manhattan. A greenhouse and water garden have been established and are meticulously maintained. What's the bottom line? Prisoners that have gone through the program have experienced a mere ten percent recidivism (repeat offenses) rate, while the rest of the facility holds at a sixty-five percent recidivism rate. This is startling and revealing news. It also helps to illustrate that prisoners working to reduce their term or pay retribution may actually have a chance to reenter mainstream society and go on to live productive lives.

None of the research I've conducted to flesh out this chapter is even modestly as optimistic. Don C. Gibbons in *Changing the Lawbreaker: The Treatment of Delinquents and Criminals* suggests that throwing more money at the problem—better facilities, higher salaries for staff, larger budgeting, etc.—will not necessarily change things. In other words, by the time a criminal reaches repeat offender status, the die is cast. Things are a little bit more optimistic with juvenile delinquents but not much. The trend is apparent, however. The sooner the problem is addressed, the better the chances at rehabilitation. The answer to treating offenders lies in taking early preventative measures. The worst thing that could possibly happen is to put would-be career criminals with hardened career criminals.

The penal system as it exists today (some would say persists) is nothing more than a vicious cycle that perpetuates itself. But unlike most cycles the amount of energy (offenders) is not fixed—it is constantly growing larger. Introducing novice offenders to veteran offenders virtually guarantees that they will move up through the ranks and become veterans themselves. So, where do the newbies get put if society can admit that placing them in existing prisoner populations is sheer folly? The revitalized CCC camps alluded to in Chapter Three come readily to mind. And where will training and instruction come from? Corporate middle management, who—not too surprisingly—constitute a middle aged work force that has been unceremoniously dumped on the streets due to job outsourcing and fat-trimming measures, come to mind. More on this in Chapter Five. The question has been asked before about these unfortunate people, victimized in corporate numbers games bordering on the behavior of the hated robber barons of the nineteenth century (and perhaps worse), shut out of their pensions and forced to void their individual retirement accounts (IRAs). Where will they go and what will they do? Herein lies the answer. They can become the leadership for the worker bees of the green revolution. Or they can become social basket cases. Albeit not of their own making, but basket cases just the same.

So let's assume for the moment that we know what to do and have a vehicle with which to do it. Is this the end of our problems? Not hardly. The rotting apple of the something-for-nothing mentality that now predominates throughout the middle generations of the bulk of American society has now penetrated to the core of its youngest members.

There's a new thing happening in grade school and high school education that is proliferating to pandemic proportions. This is the phenomenon known as "home schooling." I know about this firsthand because two of our daughters who just couldn't go with the flow of normal high school virtually forced us to put them in home schooling, the net effect being that they didn't learn much of anything.

Consider the motivation of the home schoolteacher or mentor, if you will. They oversee kids who have basically had it out with their "real" teachers and (in their minds at least) have won. Now, the budding little hard cases are tossed fresh meat on their own turf. With job perpetuation a compelling motivation, in this hopeless scenario, perhaps it's best to just pass them through the system. It's not like anything is expected of them on their SATs and if they fail their final exams we will have to deal with that when it happens. The odds are good that their "students" will wind up in juvenile hall, get pregnant, run away, or otherwise vaporize into educational thin air. If worse comes to worst, they can always opt to acquire a general education diploma (GED) which assures a minimal level of proficiency, with social skills, of course, not being a testing category. Over half won't even attempt to take the GED. They will slide into adulthood with no discernable training, skill, or motivation. Things can only get worse and they inevitably do. The schools blame the parents, the parents blame the schools, but in reality, it's an issue and manifestation of the namby pamby, everyone-has-equal-rights philosophy rampant in America today. How did things get so completely out of wack? Sure, kids have rights—basic human rights. But we have put them on a level plane with adults, and psychologists be damned, this is utter lunacy. I can speak from experience, once a child, or worse, a teenager thinks they have you by the balls, and you're not sure whether or not they do—*they do.*

How do parents take back the act of parenting? First by clamoring to have their parental rights reinstated. Not that I support physical violence, but what gives teachers, boot camp instructors, police, and/or any other non-blood-related adult the right to use it while the actual parent can't? Their hands are tied behind their backs and don't think for a New York minute that their children don't know it. Sorry to say, in a work-based parental society with little time to devote to touchy-feely emotional exploration, sometimes physical intimidation is necessary. What makes the "authorities" better parents than the parents? As crazy as this is, it isn't likely to change soon so another approach is in order, one perhaps that enlists the aid of the "authorities" as we would like to have it enlisted, as opposed to how they prefer to go about their business with our kids.

I'm enthralled with the glut of "super nanny" shows now on television postulating Hollywood's take on what it takes to be good parents. I can't help but notice that these parenting saviors are assigned screaming, romping, stomping little terrors from obviously wealthy homes. I have to wonder aloud how good ole super nanny would fare in the projects with three generations crammed into a two bedroom apartment or even in a lower middle class home where both parents have to work and can't afford child care. Go get 'em, super nanny!

So, setting super nanny and all the other supposed experts aside, what needs to be done? We need to nip prepubescent adolescent antisocial behavior in the bud. There's no better medium for instilling a sense of responsibility than work. The beauty of work is that most of it obviously needs to be done and it is just as obvious when it isn't. Tasks have an inherent beginning, middle, and end. The most important factor is completion and with this comes ownership, a sense of accomplishment, and a sense of responsibility. What kinds of jobs are available that are not too strenuous, demeaning, or difficult for kids? Virtually every form of surface environmental cleanup outside of toxic waste or that requiring heavy equipment. Recycling. Tree and flower planting. Noxious weed removal. Habitat restoration.

Voluntary outside-of-school learning programs in tandem with local business owners could illustrate the merits of mutual cooperation. This all sounds lovely but it's doubtful if even ten percent of today's problem or socially challenged kids would enter into such activities voluntarily. They must be forced to do it or encouraged in such a manner that their involvement would hold some real meaning in their lives. By "encouraged" I mean that they not be given the option of meaningless home schooling, which is nothing more than schools saying to parents, "You take them back. You must have done something wrong for them to turn out like this." To which beleaguered parents answer, "The only thing we did wrong was send them to your school."

Adults on both sides of the fence are missing the point entirely, which is that kids, especially those that are well-fed with a roof over their heads, are not that stupid and irresponsible. They have got their elders so bamboozled that we placate them by medicating them to the tune of 8 million teen aged individuals on prescription mood altering drugs. So much for spending their allowances on pot when they can score pills off their old man's and old lady's HMO. The inmates are running the asylum and as long as they make no earnest attempt at escape, we let them. The roosters are going to come home to roost in about 2015 and it isn't going to be pretty.

Who decided that the age of reason was eighteen? Why not sixteen? With the dawn of television and the computer age it isn't as if kids don't have access to all adult (including carnal) knowledge. They use this knowledge like a shield with which to manipulate their world to their own immediate benefit. It's time to get real about what constitutes responsible behavior and when to expect it. The gig is up. Children can have their childhood but teenagers past the age of sixteen need to know there will be no more free rides. If it's a sense of fairness that haunts you—let them drink (they are anyways), let them vote, let them get married, but please for the love of God let them be responsible for their own actions.

"Penitentiary" means to be housed in an establishment where one is *penitent* about an act or past behavior. What a joke! Survival in prison usually means aligning yourself with a population or segment of a population who wants nothing more than to get even with society, their jailers, and their God who rejected them. Rejection begets anger. Anger begets revenge. Revenge begets violence. It's a circular game of despair and desperation that breeds nothing more than an unwavering realization that it's okay to commit avenging crimes against one's tormentors. This, and sanctioned ongoing hatred.

Acknowledging that our prison system isn't working in today's world leads one to wonder about tomorrow's. It's a foregone conclusion that technology will continue to make our lives easier, as if the living hell it has wrought upon the earth is of no consequence. But suppose for just a moment that domestic life in the future is harder rather than easier. What then? In a world of greatly depleted fossil fuels and limited job opportunities people will be strapped for work and a way to get to work at jobs that are few and far between. What then? Crime will become more rampant. What will we do with the criminals? Is it realistic to assume that twenty, thirty, or even a higher percentage of the population can be put under house arrest? What is wrong with the prison system today will be magnified by a factor of ten tomorrow unless the country can get its arms around the problem. In this light it isn't unreasonable to assume that two entities so locked in downward spirals—the environment and the detention system—could possibly play off of and draw from each other to the mutual benefit of both.

The American environment and prison system have some remarkable similarities. The amount of crimes and criminals both must suffer is increasing. Remnants of ecosystem and remnants of what is viewed as civilized society will not long survive in isolation with no constructive input of acreage or of social training, respectively. Something must be added to this typical mix of circumstance in order to reasonably expect any form of significant change.

In *The Conscription Society: Administered Mass Organizations* by Gregory Kasza, the author makes the case that government sponsored organizations are usually set up to lend credibility, support, and future membership to political platforms. Political parties are exceedingly careful in creating the illusion of power within these organizations without actually granting it. Thus a national politically sponsored youth program could become nothing more than a puppet organization to aid some insidious political machine. Take, for example, Nazi Germany's Hitler Youth and German Labor Front, both utilized as shills for turning in Jews and being the visible face of a reign of terror. So be it. It's not going to happen in America as long as we keep our constitution, which assures a democratic form of government. Democracy, by the grace of God, still reigns in America across the platforms of both prominent parties—or at least it did.

In a country becoming dominated by the New Right's hysterical religious ideology, which is now further emboldened by the fear engendered by the events of September 11, 2001, national security has become so prominent that constitutional rights are being compromised and the citizenry is so numb that they believe that their loss is for their own good. Most of us have stopped paying attention to what's going on around us. This is very, *very* dangerous.

While the working citizenry bust their collective humps to eek out a living, the rest of society has a free ride. Welfare mothers are rewarded rather than taxed for having more kids. Middle line criminals can serve out their time at home. Kids don't have to go to real school anymore.

Has American society run completely amuck? What do we do with those living off the fat of the land?

Put them to work. Good, glorious, productive work. Save the country and help save the environment in one fell swoop. Put them to work. If our constitutional rights are being stepped on, then why not theirs? More on this later.

Put them to work. Accept nothing less. Put them to work. Conscript the manpower necessary to restore the environment. Put them to work. And save their lives in the process.

Chapter Five: Quotes
Alternative Environmental Careers

There clearly is a desperate need for professionals who are conservationists by instinct, but who care not only to preserve but to create and to manage. These persons cannot be impeccable scientists for such purity would immobilize them. They must be workmen who are instinctively interested in the physical and biological sciences, and who seek this information so that they may obtain the license to interpose their creative skills upon the land. The landscape architect meets these requirements.[15]

Design with Nature
Ian L. McHarg

A new breed of environmental pioneers is emerging on the American landscape. With the inventive genius for which Americans are justifiably proud, these trailblazers are demonstrating that we can provide for the needs of citizens today without degrading the environment to the point where future generations are unable to meet their needs. In both urban and rural settings, ecological innovators are modeling ways to log forests, grow food, raise livestock, manufacture goods, construct houses, build transportation systems, generate power, reuse materials, reduce waste, and design sustainable communities while minimizing damage to the web of life. I call these men and women "eco-pioneers" because they are modern pathfinders who are mapping out a sustainable future for our nation. With little encouragement, they are working to reverse the accelerating pace of environmental degradation so that our children and grandchildren will not be forced to live in ecologically impoverished circumstances.[16]

Eco-Pioneers
Steve Lerner

Over the past decade, unemployment rates among young people worldwide skyrocketed from 11.7 percent to a record 14.4 percent in 2003. According to the ILO an estimated 88.2 million people aged 15 to 24 were without work in 2003, accounting for nearly half the world's jobless. In the developing world—home to 85 percent young people—unemployment in this group can be nearly four times the rate amount adults.[17]

Vital Signs 2005
The Worldwatch Institute

Recycling has certainly come a long way since then. Today curbside recycling programs have spread to many communities, and fully a quarter of the trash that households dispose of gets taken to recycling centers to be made into new paper, cans, bottles—even, in one case, clothing. Yet it is clear that recycling alone cannot solve the serious environmental problems that face America and the rest of the world.[18]

The Consumer's Guide to Effective Environmental Choices
Michael Brower Ph.D.
Warren Leon Ph.D.

. . . Gradually, Kogo developed an idea he thought could make him rich—to forest Kuwait with mangroves. Fresh water was expensive in Kuwait, but there was an abundance of saltwater and desert. He started to plant mangrove trees on a small island and eventually formed a group called Action for Mangrove Reforestation. Mangroves form a rich biological zone supporting unique communities of living things at the margin of land and sea.[19]

The Sacred Balance
David Suzuki

Chapter Five

Alternative Environmental Careers

Peruse the appallingly few shelves of environmental titles at Borders and Barnes & Noble bookstores and you will find any number of doomsday texts that would cause any sane individual to ask the obvious question, "What can I do?" The members of the green revolution have been adept at quantifying the vast array of environmental problems, identifying the culprits, and placing the bulk of the blame on the mainstream of an apathetic society more intent on profiting during their lifetimes than preserving any quality of life for future generations. The problems will not go away by themselves. The culprits need to be held accountable. And the apathetic mainstream has to be won over, because it is by rousing this sleeping giant that enough money and manpower will be realized to make a dent in the myriad of screaming environmental calamities that currently seem to be falling on deaf ears.

The goal of saving the environment must be coupled with the equally important goal of saving those who wish to save the environment. This mandates that new, innovative, and financially rewarding careers be created, funded, and launched within the ever-shrinking boundaries of a rapidly diminishing window of opportunity.

Before delving into the new environmental job frontier, let's examine the old one. Traditionally, the natural sciences offered up the "O" careers, those being anything that ended in "ologist" or "ographer." These careers were defined by a strong leaning toward biology, botany, or some form of a conservation ethic. After the obligatory college education they led to jobs primarily in education and research. These jobs typically occupied the low end of the wage scale and were easily dispensed of during cyclical times of economic belt tightening. So, in the view of society, the "O" careers were looked upon as somewhat disposable in importance and marginally helpful to anyone who wished to get on a fast personal wealth track. As low tier as these education driven careers were, in the grand scheme of the overall job market, they did represent the upper tier of available environmentally slanted jobs.

Next came service oriented careers, most of which wallowed within the dictates of civil service job descriptions and seniority rather than ability based pay scales: forest rangers, park rangers, game wardens, and the like.

On the low end of the spectrum came the worker bee jobs involved in maintenance and back-breaking physical labor. Hovering around the periphery of these bottom line jobs were offbeat careers such as tour guides and whitewater river rafters.

Then there was nothing. So much for the good old days.

All of this was poised and ready to change at first with the celebration of the first Earth Day on April 22, 1970 and later when the decade of the nineties was dubbed the "green decade." Then something funny happened on the way to saving the planet. While old school environmentalists defined the scope of planetary environmental problems, and the new job frontier emerged by inference, the new school would-be environmentalists seemed little motivated and even less qualified to step up to fill the new positions. Turns out, education in America isn't what it used to be.

As the most well-educated society in our nation's history ages, simultaneously there will be a glut of retired or otherwise out of work intellectual manpower on the streets that could be utilized to the benefit of the new society—those that can't afford the high cost of education or don't fit into its rah-rah sis-cum-bah mold. Colleges and universities have become so adept at fund raising, especially acquiring direct donations and foundation money, that trade schools have been left out in the financial cold and have been unceremoniously shot down across America. For the most part, trade schools have become extinct. As recently as 2002 the California State Contractors Board stated in a newsletter that a minuscule eighteen percent of all people who initially entered four-year bachelors degree programs in the US actually graduated. What has become of the other eighty-two percent? And what is to become of the grandchildren of the babies of the baby boomers? In forty years, will America be stocked with its *least* educated workforce in our nation's post-Industrial Revolution history? We who are about to retire, or be put out to pasture, or simply break down from the weight of careers gone awry, can play a significant role in the education of the new America.

The obvious answer to the educational crisis, at least for the next two decades, is that those who are educated yet denied the opportunity to continue to apply it could easily give those that are uneducated the opportunity to achieve it. In other words, the put-out-of-work workforce could be retro-fitted to train the next-to-be-put-to-work workforce. But what would they be put to work at? A taste for physical labor is dying in America. The youth want desk jobs, most in front of computers, in air conditioned or well-heated offices. They want high salaries, generous benefits, and lots of vacation time. This trend has caused many in the construction trades to nickname them the "entitlement generation." Professional job interviewers will tell you that the tide has turned in competition for jobs. New interviewees do not view themselves as competing against each other as much as they view themselves as competing against their tight-fisted potential employers. From the viewpoint of management, if they were to hire these malcontents in waiting they would be slitting their own throats. So what they hire is not the best of the best but the least of the dissidents. If they didn't, the inmates would wind up running the asylum.

As much as I *hate* corporations and the deleterious effects they inflict upon society when they downsize and/or outsource jobs, I can somewhat understand their motives when I see the young people available to me as trainees for my tiny landscape architectural business. I invariably try to find ways to cut overhead and take on less work because of the lack of having or finding anyone who can actually help me do it. It disturbs me to no end as I see this downward spiral and often wonder what is to become of the youth of America? Those who do manage to wade through the minefields of a four-year bachelors degree program complain that nothing waits for them at the end of this trail, while those in established businesses complain that nothing is coming up the trail with enough ingenuity and motivation to cause them to take a risk on hiring them. So it can be said that B and C intellects are acquiring the too few available jobs while A intellects are acquiring jobs that are definitely beneath them, if they acquire any jobs at all. In their desire not to be taken advantage of at the outset they get locked into jobs where they can not use their acquired training and eventually lapse into a mindset of resentment and disillusionment, which is as mindless and medicating as the daytime television they now have the free time to watch.

Youth of America, take note. Work is work whether it occurs in the old job venue or on the new green frontier. Job creation does not go hand-in-hand with job ease. *No job is easy.* This is why gainful employment is referred to as a "job." That being said, the easiest job will definitely be one that you enjoy. Like Richard Leigh's and Susanna Clark's song says, "Learn to sing, like you don't need the money,"[d] and the money will come.

In *Natural Capitalism* by Paul Hawkin, Amory Lovins, and L. Hunter Lovins and again in *You Can't Eat GNP* by Eric A. Davidson, the case is repeatedly made that traditional economists fail to appropriate the value of nature and natural resources on their balance sheets. Because nature's inherent value, when depleted, is not seen as a loss on a typical profit and loss statement, the *true costs* of extractive industries are never really known or at least not until huge sums of money have been redistributed, redirected, or thoroughly hidden. The replacement of this lost natural value (if it can ever be replaced) does not fall upon those who caused the loss, meaning that someone, most likely a government entity propped up through taxation of the masses (us), will be left with the chore. In the same sing-song of either openly or circuitously subsidizing corporations, the words of country singer Travis Tritt resonate with unfaltering truth:

> *Won't you tell me if you can*
> *'Cause life's so hard to understand*
> *Why's the rich man busy dancing*
> *While the poor man pays the band.*[e]

In order of importance, in terms of the earth's impending survival, resources that are approaching catastrophic depletion proportions are:

Fresh water
Clean air
Fertile soil
Forests
Ocean fisheries

Davidson suggests that the value of topsoil, due to the forces of erosion, can be depreciated in a manner similar to building depreciation. But unlike buildings, which are viewed to have an effective life after which they are usually replaced, mankind is currently not readily capable of replacing soil and therefore it should be viewed as an invaluable resource.

How to depreciate water and air that has been despoiled past the point of immediate or time sensitive (say two years) repair is a much harder element to readily measure. In *Econation* I alluded to the carbon credit craze, which must seem like manna from heaven to those fortunate enough to be able to sell them and a virtual get-out-of-jail-free card for those who are wealthy enough to buy them. The truth of the matter is that it is nearly impossible to accurately measure use (or misuse) levels given the limitations of current technology. Even more than this, it should be remembered that American businesses have never functioned on the honor system.

Dwindling forests and ocean fisheries are, however, easily measurable, in that anyone but a blind man can see acreage being denuded of vegetation and nets devoid of fish. No hypersensitive technological equipment needed here—just common sense.

New careers should spring aplenty from the need to preserve these five major resources. Job descriptions may take some thought but job titles are readily available:

Freshwater/Groundwater Analyst
Air Purity Technician
Soil Loss/Replacement Analyst
Urban Compost Engineer
Eco-Resource Economist
Carbon Credit Analyst
Urban Forester
Rural Forester
Ocean Fisheries Replenishment Technician

Anti-enviros often point to rapid improvements in surface fresh water systems, lakes, and rivers as an affirmation that the enviros are just a bunch of hysterical, sensationalist lunatics. They use, as an example, the legend of the Cuyahoga River, which flows through the industrial corridor of Cleveland, Ohio to the shores of Lake Erie. The Cuyahoga lives in infamy for being so polluted with industrial wastes, many of which freely floated on its surface, that in early 1970 it caught fire and burned for days. Today, while still not a candidate for local swimming holes, and primarily as a result of the Clean Water Act of 1972, the Cuyahoga no longer catches fire and human feces no longer bob on the surface water of Lake Erie's beaches. The anti-enviros claim this as a success story to be filed under not-to-worry, while enviros hold out glasses to the Cuyahoga and tell them to, "drink up."

If the toxic stream of pollutants is removed from flowing waters they can cleanse themselves in a remarkably short period of time. Not so for groundwater lying in underground aquifers. Here, flows are so minimal that there is virtually no cleansing action and the underlying water table simply absorbs chemicals and wastes that find their ways into it either through leaching or injection. Once in the system they are virtually impossible to remove. One solution would to be to pump contaminated water using windmill energy, let it stand in holding ponds with successive layers of filtration, and then return it to the aquifer. This would be a monumental task performed at huge expense, but one cannot live without water. The job of Freshwater/Groundwater Analyst could well be the most important trade on the planet while other jobs could be created in windmill construction, installation, and maintenance. The same could be said of the steps required for creating the holding ponds.

Every environmental text touches on the issues of air pollution with the subsequent negative results of global warming and acid rain. While hybrid and alternative fuel cars certainly are creditable solutions for slowing the rate at which the earth will run out of fossil fuels, they won't negate the fact that humanity will exhaust fossil fuels before turning solely to alternative energy sources. Even at this, a complete atmospheric purification effort won't occur for decades, or perhaps, centuries. Only when the costs to extract fossil fuels exceed what the consuming public can pay to use them will they become obsolete. Most economists put that date between 2050 and 2070, with the surging economic growth of China representing the twenty-year wild card. So, for the foreseeable future, Koyoto Protocol or no, the earth's atmosphere will get worse. This will require the services of Air Purity Technicians with the sad irony being that they might be more correctly called Air Impurity Technicians. They will monitor air quality, work with weather forecasters in the most urban areas, and interface with the new Urban and Rural Foresters to advise them on what areas need the most immediate and heavy planting of carbon dioxide-sucking evergreen trees.

While slowing the rate of petroleum usage may allow the earth's atmosphere to somewhat cleanse itself through wind currents, it would benefit mankind to realize that it needs to get real with its ritualistic traditions of celebrating death. Elaborate funerals expend natural and capital resources that could well be put to better use. In addition, the potential compost that could be realized from the biomass of a human body goes completely unrealized. "Ashes to ashes, dust to dust," is a bunch of crap in a world that can use neither to feed itself. Biomass to compost yields some tangible benefits. In other words, I really don't care what happens to me after I'm dead and I'm certain that millions more feel the same. If I could will myself to be turned into compost after I'm dead so that I could at least give that small gift back to the earth I would do it in a heartbeat. And don't plant me six feet under. Plant me six inches under.

The number one threat to the world's immediate food supply is the startling loss of fertile soil, which is desperately needed to grow agricultural crops not only for human but also for livestock consumption. Soil loss due to water and wind erosion is causing vast areas of marginally productive cropland in sub-Saharan Africa and mid-mainland China to be converted to desert. Large swaths of separate deserts in China are merging into a super-desert. Three remediation measures to this desertification crisis immediately present themselves. First is alternate tilling techniques, most notably drill seeding, which encourages far less wind erosion in that vegetation-knitted soil is only slightly disturbed where it is slit for seed insertion. The remaining naturally vegetated undisturbed soil has enough coverage to discourage massive invasive weed growth so typical of plowing, disking, or harrowing techniques. Less weeds means less fuel used to operate cultivating machinery. Also, on center seed spacings align nicely with on center drip irrigation head spacings, which is the most efficient and water conserving irrigation practice around today. Second is (again) the use of windmills en masse across the plains, steppes, and savannahs of the world. Not only would they slow wind speed but they would have the advantage of generating electricity. Third is the recreation of topsoil through the wonders of various forms of composting, including human and animal carcasses to be decomposed in sterile subterranean pits. Vast acreages of agricultural land is not only lost to housing, roads, and parking lots, but also to graveyards.

The job of a Soil Loss/Replacement Analyst will focus on how to bridge agricultural and social issues. Religious beliefs notwithstanding, life is most valuable while living and valueless when dead. While the world threatens to approach a new mass extinction, primarily owing to the use of the by-projects of previous mass extinctions, can it really afford to ignore the potential of beneficial by-products of the yearly millions of deaths of its most prolific relatively large-scale species? This type of short-sighted thinking will shortly suffocate all of mankind.

The job of Urban Compost Engineer will be unique in that America is phobic about its excrement. We have devised elaborate sewage disposal systems that are marvels of inefficiency and monuments to misunderstanding. Most of the systems in operation in America's largest metropolitan areas are overused, fast approaching obsolescence, or in desperate need of expansion and/or repair.

Several environmentalists suggest two toilets—one for pee, one for poop. Urine could be flushed less, saving enormous quantities of water. The groady stuff processed in the self-composting toilets would require the cooperation of homeowners and business maintenance personnel to get the compost to holding locations so that it can be further processed and eventually shipped by Urban Compost Engineers. It may be viewed as a shitty job, but someone will have to do it.

Paul Hawkin has been sounding the drumbeat of natural capital longer than anyone and deserves to be taken more seriously. In a world gone mad with extraction and consumption, little thought has been given to what we are losing—until it's gone. Adam Davis has taken Hawkinesque theories a step further and champions the concept of Ecosystem Service Units (ESUs). ESUs place tangible value on not only the products of nature but also on *the work* of nature. A functioning undisturbed natural system, say a river watershed or a forested hillside, filters and purifies water or lowers carbon dioxide levels and stops erosion, respectively. These services have an economic value that could quite possibly be far greater than the value that could be gained no matter how thoroughly they were exploited.

Eco-Resource Economists will have to assign and prove these nature-driven values to traditional market-driven economists. This is frequently presented as being the difference between thinking linearly and thinking cyclically. Extraction industries represent a straight line to wealth. Money can be made until the resource is used up. Eco-businesses represent a closed loop where resources can be used over and over again and maintained at predictable sustainable levels. One guarantees extinctions while the other guarantees perpetuation. Which one makes the most sense to you?

Adam Davis and his contemporaries, most notably

Canadian forester David Brand, birthed the idea of carbon credits, which is something akin to legally printing your own money. In theory, heavily forested countries could be encouraged not to cut their timber resources because they sequester vast amounts of carbon dioxide. In response to the unrealized income the forest would have garnered, the host country would be allowed to sell carbon credits to polluting countries with no forestlands so that they could keep on polluting and not be required to enact any carbon reduction measures, or as Sony and Cher would have said, "The beat goes on."[f] This lofty aspiration of trusting in the basic goodness of business quickly became known as the "carbon credit craze" and little was expected to come of it because of ongoing questions of how to assess value and measure results.

A Carbon Credit Analyst will need to be multilingual and possess the investigative talents of an FBI agent. How, for instance, would market forces of pricing be stabilized? And how would violators to the use limits be fined and/or prosecuted? These are issues that would boggle the minds and tracing equipment of Interpol. Perhaps, if the job titles (and descriptions) of Urban Forester and Rural Forester were given serious consideration, there would be no need to delve into the mysterious inner workings of the carbon credit craze.

In 2005, after twenty-five years of being a registered landscape architect, I was called out by a hostile city employee as being irresponsible at my craft because, unlike her, I was not, "a certified arborist." This heinous shortcoming was quickly remedied when, through rigorous testing, I became an International Society of Arborists (ISA) certified arborist. This exercise opened my eyes to the burgeoning field of arboriculture. Urban Forestry is a field now offered by some of the most respected schools of forestry in the country, including renowned Syracuse University. As a field of endeavor it recognizes the vast amount of trees that now exist in our urban centers as a resource. The same can be said of the suburbs and the rural areas beyond. An issue of particular lament is the growing number of improperly planted (sited) and inappropriately located "volunteer" trees. Much effort goes toward removing these trees that could, in fact, be expended toward expanding the usable urban forest. ISA does, in fact, recognize a separate branch of the industry by certifying Utility Specialists for working on trees inappropriately placed under power lines— and it's a big part of the industry, with large contracts extended by utility companies every year. The costs for this are, of course, passed on to their consumers.

Besides trees that are economic and safety nuisances because of location issues, a tree in the city is worth its weight in gold. One can only assume that a tree in the suburbs is worth its weight in silver. In populous areas, trees are what subliminally connect us to nature. As an added benefit, they sequester airborne carbon dioxide. The field of forestry no longer exists solely in the national forests, which is good because the Bush administration may yet level them all. The jobs of Urban Forester and Rural Forester will certainly grow in importance in the coming decades. They will rely heavily on a partnership with the nation's citizenry. For every tree taken the citizenry needs to plant ten more, and if the only place that they own on which to do this is their front and back yards then that is where the battle must be fought. Let's at least take back the density of our forests one tree at a time, wherever and whenever we can plant them.

While many planners, myself included, felt that the oceans of the world could be enlisted to feed the peoples of the world, to date we have been sorely mistaken. Our ocean fisheries, once looked upon as vast and limitless, are now collapsing. Dear Lord, where do we turn to now? We obviously have to relieve overharvesting pressures on these stressed oceanic fisheries by enacting moratoriums with stiff penalties levied against violators. Seaside fish and shrimp farms have proved to be poor substitutes for the real thing, in that occupants of enclosed pens literally float in their own fecal soup. Salmon, in particular, don't respond well to artificial growing methods, leading several of California's coastal indigenous peoples to form the "Salmon Nation" and call for fish farming of salmon to be outlawed.

Perhaps the issue of harvesting the oceans (at least for the short term) is mired in the desire to harvest just the animal species. Plant species, especially plankton, could be reared at far greater pound per square unit of ocean water ratios than any animal species. Plankton, of course, is not nearly as tasty as fish, but to a starving world, it may be just tasty enough. And then there's the potential of the estuaries and protected coastal areas to produce harvests from halophytes, those plants that thrive in brackish water. David Suzuki in *The Sacred Balance: Rediscovering Our Place in Nature* tells the story of Motohiko Kogo, a man who wishes to enrich planetary food stores through massive seaside plantings of mangrove trees. Even tastier than plankton, say I. The career of Ocean Fisheries Replenishment Technician must merge the intellectual inquisitiveness of Jacques Yves Cousteau with the tenacious survival instincts of a Great Plains family farmer, for I still believe that in some way, shape, or form, my words written in *Environmental Cognizance, The sea, however, must serve a higher purpose, for soon, very soon, 2020 soon, it will have to feed us all,*[20] will ring true.

The environmental mantra of reduce, reuse, and recycle

could use a few new "r" words—restore, renovate, revitalize, etcetera, tacked on to it. Jobs could be created to further the purpose of any given "r" word.

We've just touched the tip of the iceberg. In *Econation* I quoted liberally from Lester R. Brown's *Eco-Economy,* in which he described at least ten emerging job opportunities that could provide rewarding careers for those bold enough to reach out and seize them. The fact of the matter is that the subtitle "eco" or "green" could be tacked in front of just about any conventional job title. Eco-Accountant, Eco-Attorney, Green Machinist, Green Butcher, Baker, Candlestick Maker.

What's important to know is that work is work and the careers that await the youth of America on the environmental frontier will require the efforts of those willing to work the hardest. The emerging workforce of the green revolution should know that, in environmentalism, hard work is not its own reward—it results in the reward of the earth to its inhabitants, especially those that have finally realized that it is better to give than to receive.

And now—get to work!

Chapter Six: Quotes
Creating Environmental Land Trusts and Partnerships and Green Investing

According to Pinchot, the conservation issue is a moral issue, and the heart of it is this: For whose benefit shall our natural resources be conserved—for the benefit of us all, or for the use and profit of a few? This truth is so obvious and the question itself so simple that the attitude toward conservation of any man in public or private life indicates his stand in the fight for public rights.[21]

President Theodore Roosevelt's Conservation Legacy
W. Todd Benson

How fragmentedly we live, in broken families, crippled communities, landscapes chopped into pieces; we become disconnected from the sources of our survival, the land and each other, alienated from the earth and from things that hold meaning. I had come back to live in the stories of my people, to live a life that made sense. Somehow it wasn't working. Too much had been lost. Instead of wholeness I was finding scraps. Day after day I stared my life in the face, examining what I was missing. I was desperately lonely in the fragmentation, which was as much grief as anything, hanging on to remnants of beauty, spirit, art, touch, truth. For months I had felt cut off from the landscape of poetry. What else to call magic and spirit and truth? I had found only glimpses. Bitterly now I admitted that I had been torn apart in my homeland, these coastal plains, separated from intimacy, cut off from much of what I knew myself to be, waiting for the chance to flourish, to grow again. Waiting for what might not happen—for the logging to stop and the land to heal, and simultaneously for the communities that depended on the land to function again.[22]

Wild Card Quilt
Janisse Ray

Nature conservation has largely been an ad hoc process. Tracts of land have been protected from development for their scenic value, or because they contain impressive concentrations of wildlife, or less often because they harbor rare species or notable biological diversity. This ad hoc approach to biological conservation has left Canada, the United States, Mexico, and most other countries with highly fragmented systems of parks and reserves in which some elements of the native biota are over represented and others are not represented at all. Not only are most of the protected areas too small, but they are also isolated from other protected areas by agricultural lands, freeways, industrial zones, or other unnatural environments that are inimical to the large majority of native species . . .

A large body of research in conservation biology has shown that maintaining ecological structure, diversity, and resilience demands strict, large-scale protection of entire ecosystems (see Noss and Cooperrider 1994). There is evidence that roughly 50 percent of the land in a region needs to be protected in systems of linked core areas if the goal of preventing further anthropogenic extinctions is to be achieved (Soulé and Sanjayan 1998).[23]

Continental Conversation
Michael E. Soule
John Treborgh

The nation's more than 1,500 nonprofit land trusts have conserved millions of acres of wildlife habitat, farms, ranches, forests, watersheds, recreation areas and other important lands. The continued success of land trusts depends both on public confidence in, and support of the conservation efforts of these organizations, and on building conservation programs that stand the test of time. It is every land trust's responsibility to uphold this public trust and to ensure the permanence of its conservation efforts.[24]

Land Trust Standards and Practices
Land Trust Alliance

Chapter Six

Creating Environmental Land Trusts and Partnerships and Green Investing

Janisse Ray waxes eloquently about fragmentation in *Wild Card Quilt: Taking a Chance on Home.* She makes the point that perhaps we accept fragmentation of our open space, public lands, and wild lands because we accept fragmentation of our personal lives. When you consider the staggering negative statistics related to divorce, broken homes, deadbeat dads, single mothers, children cast to the wind by parents unwilling more than unable to care for them, then you would have to agree that this fragmentation theory is more than a mere point—it makes a compelling argument.

The problem with the environmental movement, especially in America, is that the people it could help the most—the SUV fossil fuel consuming, overeating, big-home-in-the-suburbs, the-more-kids-the-better populace—is in a state of denial just as real and just as damaging over time as the worst practicing alcoholic or drug addict. Until there's a national intervention things are bound to get worse. There's a parallel alright between the fragmentation in our personal lives and the fragmentation we allow in the environment.

Mankind has passed the omega point on the world's fuel

usage chart, paying even less attention to it than we would to a speed limit sign on an open stretch of highway in rural Montana. Of the two trillion barrels of oil estimated to be on earth when Henry Ford fired up his first quadracycle in 1896, it's estimated that just over half is gone. That was 110 years ago right? So why worry until the first quarter of the twenty-second century? Worry, worry a lot, because the exponential increase in population growth has concurrently meant an exponential increase in automobiles. Cut the number in half and we arrive at a date of 2060 or in quarter and the world will be slamming on the brakes in 2030. With China aspiring to the prominence of the world's number one economy, it could easily be 2025 and there's an outside chance that a small contingent could be walking in my funeral procession. Most experts put the magic numbers between 2050 and 2070 backed up by no other facts than they're experts. Even at 2070 our children and grandchildren will live in a world dramatically different than ours. Going back to this fragmentation theory it's possible that the family unit will be better off if for no other reason than it won't be as easy to pack up and motor away from each other.

Cities and their hinterlands of the not-too-distant future will have to rely on agricultural goods and other food stores (e.g. livestock) from sources in their immediate region. People won't be able to travel as much anymore and those that do will find it hugely expensive and cumbersome. Three hundred years removed from when he envisioned it, Thomas Jefferson may yet get his agrarian society—if there is enough fertile land left.

While, on the surface, it may appear that the environment may be better off without the oil-guzzling automobile, in other areas it could be demonstrably worse off. We will become a wood burning society in order to heat our homes and cook our food. Rail systems, especially those providing cross continental travel, may well have to revert back to steam. So the possibility exists that suburbia may turn back to victory gardens, and our few remaining forests will be leveled for fuel consumption. The former occurrence definitely good and the latter definitely bad. The built landscape will look dramatically different and the natural landscape will be dramatically threatened. In this survival scenario where does the environment fit in? I referred to a patchwork quilt of preserved land in *Econation* and while it appears destined to become patchier it still needs to be sewn together. This being the case, there is no better time to start than right now. To this end, various environmental organizations in America are vying for individual landowners to will their property over to them so that it can be managed for the good of the environment after their deaths. This is termed "direct giving." It has no strings attached as the soon-to-be mentioned trusts frequently do. Whether by direct giving or by setting up a trust the patchwork quilt concept remains the same. With enough patches, so the theory goes, the quilt of environmental preservation can be sewn. A noble goal to be sure, but one based on flawed thinking. Animals need a lot of habitat, some biologists believe up to fifty percent of the surface area of any given location.

Its doubtful if half of American soil will be given over to environmental purposes. Worldwide, land has been compromised since European contact and precious little of it, less than two percent, exists in a pristine state. As of 2000 approximately seven percent of the world's total land mass had been set aside for the purposes of habitat preservation as parks, reserves, open space, etc. It should be noted that these areas are predominately not untouched by the hand of man. Many, in fact, are utilized for the sake of tourism and people are actually encouraged to frequent them. So how do we get from seven percent to fifty percent? We don't. We admit that unless the world becomes significantly (perhaps catastrophically) depopulated we are dealing with compromised levels of environmental purity. Personally, I think its God's mercy that we are able to look and see and feel the nature that is left. Never mind, for the moment, what is gone and revel in what still remains. Thank God for that and now let's try to increase it. Maybe we can get to twenty percent set aside land by the time the world runs out of fossil fuels. Then, with mankind closing in closer to urban centers, areas that were once countryside or countryside bordering on wilderness will revitalize themselves. One hundred-and-fifty to two hundred years hence, a fifty percent natural habitat goal may very well be achievable. The point is we have to start somewhere *right here right now.*

The vehicle most frequently employed in the United States for acquiring and setting aside habitat is a nonprofit land trust. These are organizations that operate independently of government, which is good because if we depended on government to address environmental issues we would be waiting for a longer time than the earth has. While the Audubon Society, Nature Conservancy, and the Sierra Club, the "big three," are the most well known organizations that land owners enter into trusts with, there are 1,500 smaller yet credible organizations that are making significant contributions to preserving and saving the environment. The Trust for Public Land works from a slightly different angle and acquires land for the purposes of historical preservation and human enjoyment. In all, 9.3 million acres of ground, an area slightly smaller than Massachusetts and New Jersey combined, our forty-fifth and forty-sixth largest states respectively, have been set aside. Considering that this is a private non-governmental effort, it is impressive. There is still a long way to go.

With the largest segment of the American population aging more or less simultaneously, the babies born of the baby boom will lose their boom and plummet headlong into old age, prompting the field of estate planning to grow by leaps and bounds. Fear of probate causes people to do strange things. Probate is quite possibly one of the most misunderstood functions of dying and engenders as much terror in people's hearts as an audit from the IRS. When someone passes on they either die testate (with a will) or intestate (without a will). Assuming that one has a will it does not necessarily guarantee that the probate court will find it valid. If someone does not have a will, the probate court is put upon to determine how their estate will be appropriated. This follows the dictates of state law, which is fair enough, but it should be noted that whenever a government entity is put in the position to determine fairness it will be imminently fair to itself above all else. The government entity without fail will take the lion's share of any estate that falls into its treacherous hands, so anyone of means that cares about her/his family should take every precaution not to die intestate. This being said it should also be noted that most of us have a fear of probate, which is entirely unwarranted in light of the fact that one can't get blood out of a turnip. In other words, no matter how much a little is divided up it will ultimately lead to the acquisition of little.

The dreaded "death tax," which we fall all over ourselves to avoid, has an exemption for any estate that is worth less than a million dollars. This probably rules out seventy-five percent of the aging population that is about to pass on. The IRS promulgates rules and regulations, which are ever moving targets. Nowhere is this more true than with the estate tax. Some people try to avoid estate tax by virtually giving their estate away during their lifetime. The IRS gets them either coming or going. They're determined to get their cut. They foil this tactic of the giftor by inflicting the *gift tax* on the gif-tee. Trying to outsmart the IRS is like playing goalie for the dart team—there's no way you're not going to get stuck.

If a person's estate qualifies to be subject to the estate tax, the rate of taxation for the next five years is roughly forty-five percent—a stern measure and gaping bite indeed. But the cut off amount for the death tax is ever changing. The estate tax exemption in 2006 is two million dollars and rises to a whopping $3,500,000 in 2009. In 2010 the estate tax goes away altogether, but before we all get misty-eyed over the generosi-ty of government it should be noted that, "Vengeance is mine sayeth the Lord," (and the federal government). 2010 is mere-ly a one-year hiatus and then the exemption ceiling falls back to one million dollars. It appears that the feds are giving us ample reason to die en masse in 2010, which could go a long way to right the listing Social Security ship that is rapidly tak-ing on water. With laws and guidelines like these what is any sane person to do? Remember that no probate equates to no estate tax being levied. Therefore, it behooves people of means to avoid probate like the plague. This is most frequently accomplished through setting up real estate trusts.

The concept of trust land has been with us a long time. Native American Indian Reservations, for an example, are pro-tected from outside encroachment by a trust patent issued by the federal government. Trusts are a convention of real estate law. There is a trustor, that is the individual or entity giving the land away or entering into some form of an agreement to control how it will be used in the future. The trustor assigns a trustee to execute the dictates of the trust agreement. Sometimes the trustor and the trustee are the same person until death makes this an unsuitable arrangement. Often the trustee is an environmental organization. This trustee (environmental organization) carries out the wishes of the trustor and caters to the needs of the beneficiary. Who the beneficiary is can be a cloudy issue. Ultimately it is the environment, without question. However, just when or how much the environment benefits is a matter of much conjecture. This is because of the level of trust the trustor has in the trustee and what his/her directives are. There are many ways to set land aside for the enjoyment of future generations. The simplest is to just give the land over to the environmental organization and let them do with it what they will. This could easily entail them selling it and using the proceeds to purchase more environmentally (from a biodiversity standpoint) desirable acreage. A limited trust or a conservation easement comes with some strings attached, which facilitates the needs of a trustor. Say an individual has worked her/his land for a number of years and wants to keep it in their family, but in the state (use level) that it currently is in. They could stipulate that the land never be sold, never be developed, and never be clear cut, etc. They could set it up so that their children and direct descendants of their children would always be allowed to live on and work the acreage, the only limitation being that they could never sell it. In families (like mine) where rival siblings harbor divergent opinions about what to do with their inherited land, this could be a godsend. They would always have a place to live and no sibling could ever get a financial upper hand on the other.

Estate Planning for Dummies by N. Brian Caverly, Esq. and Jordan S. Simon delves into the nature of trusts at length.

A trust that is set up and can be managed while the trustor/trustee is still alive is called an intervivos trust. A trust that goes into effect after the trustor/trustee dies is termed a testamentary trust. Without question, a trustor/trustee has far greater ongoing control over an intervivos trust by virtue of the fact that he/she is still alive to control it.

Intervivos, or living trusts, are witnessed and can be amended if rewitnessed. Testamentary, or dead trusts, on the other hand, are not witnessed and cannot be changed because there is no one to testify as to the validity of the changes in comparison to the trustor's original wishes. Living trusts, as a vehicle to affect certain trustor wishes, can be extremely innovative and flexible.

As with all things, trusts are not infallible as things can and do go wrong. First, the trustor may refuse to die with the net affect being that benefits fail to trickle down to the beneficiaries and they become disgruntled. Or the trustor dies too soon, throwing a trustee who hasn't had adequate time to prepare for the once impending but now immediate task into the lurch. Or, horror of all horrors, the beneficiary(s) are undeserving or unworthy of what the trustor has ultimately bestowed upon them. *Don't give pearls to swine. They will trample the pearls and turn and attack you* (Matthew 7:6). Or in your absence (because you're dead), they will attack (or squander) the bounty of the very estate they were left with. Setting up an estate trust can be like juggling chain saws. Somewhere along the line you are virtually guaranteed to lacerate flesh while attempting to please everyone. In circumstances such as this it is best to enlist the services of an experienced real estate/trust attorney. They're experts at equitably dispensing animosity and outrage.

With the problems associated with executing the intent of

a standard estate, one has to wonder if an estate set up on the behalf of the environment is easier or harder to effectuate. As with other life tasks it depends on initial basic motivations and how realistic the expected results of those motivations in action are. The vagaries and vanity of people can thwart even the best intentions and we all know where these lead to. Helping the environment, however, is certainly a win/win situation. It won't turn on you and disappoint you from the grave, and in the final analysis, more people than you could have possibly imagined are helped.

Why is it important to preserve nature at all? Is mankind really that altruistic? If we can't help nature for nature's sake, let's do it for our own. For the last two decades E. O. Wilson, Harvard's premier evolutionary biologist, has held forth the theory of biophilia, which puts into words what many of us already knew. Wilson contends that humans that have been born in and that have ready access to nature build up an affinity for it that gets hardwired into their psyche. A relationship with nature can heal ailments more quickly, calm and restore one's sense of well being, and basically instill a sense of inner peacefulness. Landscape architect/land planner Ian McHarg was hitting home on the same theory from a different angle as far back as 1969 when he published *Design With Nature* and suggested that the deviant behavior evident in purposefully overcrowded laboratory rats may indeed move up the food chain and be manifested in mankind. The next three decades bore this out with a vengeance. So humans are affected by their natural surroundings or lack thereof. Is this any shocking enlightenment?

Not too surprisingly, psychologists jumped on the bandwagon of this man-benefits-in-the-presence-of-nature revelation. In 1995, Theodore Roszak, Mary E. Gomes, and Allen

D. Kanner published *Ecopsychology: Restoring the Earth Healing the Mind,* which was a compilation of some of the viewpoints of some of the best minds in the profession. Tried it. Could only get halfway through it. It never ceases to amaze me how cognizant we are of our fragile personal mental health problems, the degree of which are whipped into a frenzy by psychologists and only assuaged by some form of inner growth or payment of the all important consultation fee. Patient, heal thyself! Dispense with ecobabble and realize this one kernel of truth so key to the success of the green revolution: *people are animals and animals need space.* If we can't count on our government to provide that space, then we are going to have to do it ourselves. To be fair to government, perhaps in this case their hands really are tied. What would happen if the government suddenly decided to gobble up land by whatever means necessary, even by enforcing eminent domain? The populace would rise up in arms. The problem with mandated environmental programs is that they smack of socialism, which has always been a dirty word to Americans even if it does present a methodology for a larger and cleaner environment.

I don't think we can count on government to protect our natural resources or natural areas much longer. I think Social Security will be defunct in my lifetime. I feel our national forests will come under siege. As environmentalists strive to create a patchwork quilt of open space in whatever manner they can, the moths of population growth, governmental hypocrisy, fossil fuel depletion, and being denied the lifestyle to which we all feel we are accustomed and entitled to will almost immediately start to gnaw on its edges. The patchwork quilt will never be completed nor should it be viewed that it ever could be. Members of the green revolution, know this: *you are at war.* Whatever land is gained will come under attack to be taken back by the corporations, the New Right, and anyone else who sees a quick buck to be made. Knowing this as we know the backs of our own hands, it is imperative that we lay our well-intended hands on as much land as we can get, keep acquiring it, and never believe that the environment could ever have enough. This is a lock jawed death grip battle for survival of the planet. It is an eternal struggle and as long as mankind inhabits the planet it will never end.

Forming land partnerships with family, friends, and neighbors may be a simpler and more effective strategy. On a local, grassroots level, the subtle nuances of community customs and traditions can be interwoven into the patchwork quilt with more sensitivity and flair than the national organizations could ever hope to achieve.

Business scholars will tell you that a partnership is a precariously terrible form of business. First, is the fact that many partnerships are formed for the wrong reasons, usually to quell doubt, alleviate loneliness, or galvanize friendships and not because the participants actually need each other. Secondly, the law is quite specific that the debts and obligations of your partner(s) immediately become yours. So why would anyone go near a land partnership? Because they truly do *need each other.* Because aiding the cause of the dwindling environment outweighs fears of financial ruin. Because it may be the fastest way, albeit the only way, to get the job done. That's why.

There are safer forms of partnerships. Contiguous landowners can join together to form land or homeowners associations, which can write land use standards, including environmental protections, into their codes, covenants, and restrictions (CCRs). These could prescribe allowable percentages of building coverage, amount of open space, allowable usage levels for resources such as water, and an acceptable plant palette, of which a certain percentage should be indigenous.

If citizens of any given community don't want to enter into anything as threatening as a partnership or restricting as an association, they could still band together to write land use standards and lobby to have them incorporated into town, city, county, state, or national building codes and zoning ordinances. The key requisite for these measures being environmental protection and/or restoration.

Green investing will become more commonplace by the end of this decade. The editors of *E/The Environmental Magazine* have put out a book entitled *Green Living: The E Magazine Handbook for Living Lightly on the Earth*. In it they discuss all the usual subjects with several new and innovative perspectives and one unusual subject—green investing, to which they affix the acronym SRI, socially responsible investing. While treasury bills and certificates of deposit are the safest long-term investments, having a superior interest rate to that of savings or money market accounts, they do have some drawbacks. A treasury bill in some small way *does* help to prop up America's war machine and other military spending. What is the institution issuing a certificate of deposit actually investing in? This question has prompted some banks and credit unions to reveal their true colors by divulging the environmentally friendly businesses they invest in and eliminating those that are ecologically damaging from their portfolios. *E Magazine* cites Shore Bank Pacific is a model "green" bank. Others are jumping on the bandwagon. Beware of supporting loan funds and trusts unless you believe strongly in their mission statement because they *are not* federally insured.

Environmentally and socially responsible companies are popping up all over the country and some are now floating themselves on the stock market. Stocks are and always have been a crapshoot. While huge profits can be reaped in startling short periods of time so too can immense losses. While the stock market crash of 1929 is far removed from the minds of today's corporate raiders and business pirates, there is nothing in the structure of today's stock market that unequivocally guarantees that a cataclysmic crash couldn't happen again.

Long term (five year) bonds, particularly US Treasury bonds, are safe, while tax-free municipal bonds benefit people in higher tax brackets. Again it behooves the green investor to check into just what purpose or program these municipal bonds were issued for.

Investment groups wishing to remove some of the volatility of individual stocks developed a way to hedge their bets by devising mutual funds, which are groups of stocks housed under one roof. Risk is spread but reward is diluted. Mutual funds do not approach the soaring highs that a successful individual stock may, nor do they plummet as low. *E Magazine* cites Winslow Green Growth Fund and Green Century Balanced Fund as two of the very best mutual funds. Others are sure to follow. *It should be understood that all investing is a balancing act between risk and reward.*

If you consider your purchases to be investments then there is quite a bit you can do to lend a hand to the cause of environmentalism. This is especially true in the area of most people's largest investments—their home and their car.

Homes built with environmentally in-tune building materials and weather sealed to significantly save on energy losses are certainly a good thing. Nothing in home construction is going to aid the environmental cause more than *lessening the square footage of homes.* This was amply alluded to in *Econation.* Hybrid cars are beginning to flourish and they definitely do increase gas mileage. More helpful, in the short term, to the environment is America's national awakening to the gross fuel inefficiency of sports utility vehicles, unaffectively known as SUVs. Without advocating violence or monkey wrenching in any form, offenders with mileage ratings under twenty-five GPM have to go. While President George W. Bush hammers home on national security, and our eyes cross with the movements of the color alert code, an even more immediate issue of national security—fossil fuel consumption—goes unaddressed while the warning of Chili Palmer in *Be Cool* goes unheeded. James Howard Kunstler refers to this national attention deficit disorder as, *Sleep walking into the future.*[32]

Virtually every purchase has some semblance of an environmental consequence. We need to become more aware of what we are putting into our bodies. America is the most obese country on earth and with this gluttonous food and beverage consumption come inherit fats, growth hormones, and toxins. Social commentator/comedian Bill Maher notes that stadium, arena, and mass transit seating in America has all been *widened* in the last ten years. This is, of course, to accommodate the prodigious amount of ever expanding buttocks that are sweeping the nation. "Folks, it's the food," states Maher as he expounds upon the multitudinous antacid, bloating, and heartburn commercials proliferating during the evening news. Maher drives home the point that the food is so readily undigestable that it is struggling to get out of our bodies by whatever means necessary. And as for our bodies, Maher states, "The call is coming from inside the house." Consuming organically grown food is perhaps the best investment we can make for ourselves. After all, we have to be of sound mind and sound body to make sound environmental decisions in the future.

The consuming public is not powerless in effecting positive environmental change. The free enterprise system is based on a *market driven economy*. While the corporations want to charge what the market will bear, consumers can fight back with their pocket books. Acquire *The Consumer's Guide to Effective Environmental Choices: Practical Advice from the Union of Concerned Scientists* to dig deeper into this issue.

Stock purchases in the new environmental businesses, or in established businesses for that matter, equate to a portion of ownership in that particular company, no matter how small. With ownership comes voting and with voting comes change.

The leadership of the emerging green businesses represents some of the finest and original thinking intellects in the country. Paul Hawkin of Smith and Hawkin, an outdoor furniture company, is an excellent example. Is it any wonder that these new environmental businesses frequently outperform existing environmentally damaging and resource depleting businesses? Again credit *E Magazine* for pointing out that new green businesses, in mirroring their beliefs, are less wasteful, more efficient, and don't get sued nearly as often as conventional businesses. What's to sue? Who are they damaging?

As the United States attempts to metamorphose from the world's most extractive and consuming country to a sustainable society, fresh, out-of-the-box thinking and problem solving methodologies will be at a premium.

Investing in the future will necessitate investing in this new leadership and the products and services they bring to the table—*now.*

Chapter Seven: Quotes
Renaturalizing and Restoring Cities and Suburbs

As we have seen, the city has undergone many changes during the last five thousand years; and further changes are doubtless in store. But the innovations that beckon urgently are not in the extension and perfection of physical equipment: still less in multiplying automatic electronic devices for dispersing into formless suburban dust the remaining organs of culture. Just the contrary: significant improvements will come only through applying art and thought to the city's central human concerns, with a fresh dedication to the cosmic and ecological processes that enfold all being. We must restore to the city the maternal, life-nurturing functions, the autonomous activities, the symbiotic associations that have long been neglected or suppressed. For the city should be an organ of love; and the best economy of cities is the care and culture of men.[25]

The City in History
Lewis Mumford

The life of cities is of two kinds—one is public and social, extroverted and interrelated. It is the life of the streets and plazas, the great parks and civic spaces and the dense activity and excitement of the shopping areas. This life is mostly out in the open in the great urban spaces, where crowds gather and people participate in the exciting urban interrelationships, which they seek as social human beings. It is the life of sidewalk cafes and museums and water-front activities, of theatre-going and night clubs at night; the public city, bustling, active and exciting.

There is, too, a second kind of life in the city—private and introverted, the personal, individual, self-oriented life, which seeks quiet and seclusion and privacy. This private life has need for open spaces of a different kind, which will be described in the next chapter. It needs enclosure and quiet, removal from crowds and a quality of calm and relaxation.

The city should respond to both needs and both kinds of activity for they are equally important parts of the urban environment we are seeking.[26]

Cities
Lawrence Halprin

Is downtown dead? Can it live again? Most accepted rules of thumb about downtown are wrong. About why it died—and how to bring it back. About why retail and manufacturing left—and how to bring them back. About what constitutes rebirth—and how to make it happen. Zoning, building and fire codes, traffic, parking, signage standards, market strategies, financial formulas, and economic development strategies tend to discourage or prevent the right things from happening and guarantee that the wrong things will. Doing it right today and tomorrow means shattering the rules of yesterday—especially the rules of city planning and transportation—that persist today.[27]

Cities Back from the Edge
Roberta Brandee Guatz
With Norman Mintz

And all around the planet, the "typical" surroundings of vast numbers of people are radically changing character: Until recently, a large majority of the world's population lived in villages. Less than a decade from now, a small majority of the world's population (52 percent) will live in cities. And a hundred years from now, as many as 90 percent of all people may live in cities, and even today many city residents have little or no access to either wilderness areas or farming.[28]

The Experience of Place
Tony Hiss

But whatever its shortcomings as a place to live, the suburban subdivision was unquestionably a successful product. For many, it was a vast improvement over what they were used to. The houses were spacious compared to city dwellings, and they contained modern conveniences. Air, light, and a modicum of greenery came with the package. The main problem with it was that it dispensed with all the traditional con-

110

nections and continuities of community life, and replaced them with little more than cars and television.[29]

The Geography of Nowhere
James Howard Kunstler

The old suburban dream is increasingly out of sync with today's culture. Our household makeup has changed dramatically, the work place and work force have been transformed, average family wealth is shrinking, and serious environmental concerns have surfaced. But we continue to build post World War II suburbs as if families were large and had only one breadwinner, as if the jobs were all downtown, as if land and energy were endless, and as if another lane on the freeway would end traffic congestion.[30]

The Next American Metropolis
Peter Calthorpe

For children to live only in contact with concrete and steel and wires and wheels and machines and computers and plastics, to seldom experience any primordial reality or even to see the stars at night, is a soul deprivation that diminishes the deepest of their human experiences.[31]

The Great Work: Our Way into the Future
Thomas Berry

The future is now here for a living arrangement that had no future. We spent all our wealth acquired in the twentieth century building an infrastructure of daily life that will not work very long into the twenty-first century. It's worth repeating that suburbia is best understood as the greatest misallocation of resources in the history of the world. There really is no way to fully calculate the cost of doing what we did America, even if you try to tote up only the monetary costs (leaving out the social and environmental ones). Certainly it is somewhere up in the tens of trillions of dollars when one figures in all the roads, and highways, all the cars and trucks built since 1905, the far-flung networks of electricity, telephone, and water lines, the scores of thousands of housing sub-

divisions, a similar number of strip malls, thousands of regional shopping malls, power centers, big-box pods, hamburger and pizza shacks, donut shops, office parks, central schools, and all the other constructed accessories of that life. I have described it at length in other books. The question now is: What will become of it?

Suburbia has a tragic destiny. More than half the U.S. population lives in it. The economy of recent decades is based largely on the building and servicing of it. And the whole system will not operate without liberal and reliable supplies of cheap oil and natural gas. Suburbia is going to lose its value catastrophically as it loses its utility. People who made bad choices and invested the bulk of their life savings in high-priced suburban houses will be in trouble. They will be stuck with houses in unfavorable locations—surrounded by similar dysfunctional artifacts of sprawl—and if they are lucky enough to sell them at all, they will only create an identical set of tragic problems for some greater fool of a buyer. Even fantastic bargains will end up being no bargain. The loss of hallucinated wealth will be stupendous and the disruption of accustomed suburban logistics will be a nightmare for those stuck there. Perhaps a greater question is this: Will the collapse of suburbia as a viable mode of living tear the nation apart, both socially and politically? [32]

The Long Emergency
James Howard Kunstler

Chapter Seven

Renaturalizing and Restoring Cities and Suburbs

Let's examine empirically how we feel about cities. These outward or subliminal feelings probably are based upon where one grew up, how one matured, and the evolving lifestyle one experiences as he/she goes from child, single adult, married, divorced, parent, middle-aged, retired, elderly, dead.

When I was young I had a deathly fear of cities. I was, of course, from a sparsely populated rural area in western New York where the streets were rolled up at night and about the only reliable form of nightly entertainment was the dependable television. There were constant news reports of robberies, hold-ups, shoot-outs, and murders that were occurring in Buffalo, that hotbed of sin sixty miles to the north yet, in my reality, somewhere on another planet.

In 1970 I attended junior college at the State University of New York at Cobleskill in the famed Catskill Mountains, which was located in a town even smaller than mine. Due to the state drinking age of eighteen, and the school's two to one student ratio (women to men) I came to view Cobleskill as heaven on earth. At least half of the student body was from New York City and its surrounding suburbs or Long Island, which, at that time, was becoming a gargantuan suburb. I considered them all city kids and quickly learned that the city kids and I were different. Not that this was all bad. To a country bumpkin such as myself rubbing shoulders with hip, jaded contemporaries taught me lessons a counterculture quasi-hippy in the making needed to learn.

In the spring of 1971, a bunch of us jumped on a bus headed for Washington, DC where, as rabid Viet Nam War protestors, we were hell bent on a showdown with then US President Richard Milhous Nixon. Tricky Dick characteristically left town before the 500,000 strong protest gained fanatical inertia. As I roamed the capital area looking about for whom or what to overcome, I couldn't help but notice that this part of the city had an *aura*. The radial axis of its streets, its Lincoln and Washington monuments, and the Capital Building itself were literally breathtaking. DC was a city of circumstance. Important things happened here and everything seemed to stand a little straighter, a little more proud.

In the summer of '71, similar to most college students of the era, I was working by day and carousing by night when a friend I had met the previous semester at Cobleskill unexpectedly dropped in to tempt me to join him on a jaunt to Boston and New York City before facing the hideous academic obligations of our impending sophomore year. With such tortures to the human spirit imminent, I quickly decided to join him. My parents were none too pleased when we gored ourselves like condemned men at their dinner table, which was part of our master plan of not to spend much money on frivolities like food on our journey. So with a newfound wanderlust, and sixty bucks in my pocket, I stuck out my thumb and set out to see two of the great cities of the eastern seaboard. This was an episode that was to have a profound effect on my selection of landscape architecture as a career.

Boston oozed history. It literally haunted me that I could feel so deeply events that had occurred almost two hundred years prior, but feel them I did. Or perhaps it was the effects of my first trip on mescaline.

New York emanated an intimidating scale and was such a frenzy of activity that I just had to sit back and take it all in with my mouth agape. Central Park, designed in 1858 by Frederick Law Olmstead, the father of landscape architecture, illustrated to me beyond a shadow of a doubt what a breath of fresh air open and wooded space can be in such an urban setting. In short, it humbled me. Olmstead, it should be noted, died in a sanitarium, which was not a good omen for one soon to be inflected with other career related curses.

Leaving comfortable Cobleskill for the confines of Washington State University in the fall of '72 necessitated a cross-country trip in my first automobile (which I drove like a hot rod), where I would traverse cities such as Cleveland, Detroit, and massive Chicago. The freeway skirted these cities, predictably along their very worst parts, causing me to fear for my repressed peckerwood life and dictating that I gas up well ahead of or well behind them.

Washington State was ten times larger than Cobleskill. The state drinking age was twenty-one, and the student ratio slid horrifically toward the male end of the spectrum. After a week I hated the place and needed an outlet for pent-up cross-country hormones and east/west culture shock. Upon enrolling in the fledgling program of landscape architecture a bunch of us students were herded onto a bus for a class field trip headed for Seattle and Vancouver, BC. Emotionally, it quite possibly saved my life.

In comparison to Washington DC, I was not much impressed with Seattle. It appeared to be a city crammed onto a hillside rather than working with the natural lay of the land. There was a noticeable mix of cultures, especially Orientals, which added some spice. It's saving grace, Pioneer Square, designed by renowned landscape architects Jones and Jones, was as well done a space as I would ever encounter in my career. The horse chestnuts along fraternity row at the University of Washington were massively scaled and in a riot of full fall color, which made the place all the more impressive although, as a Cougar, I really hate to admit this.

The next day we crossed the border into Canada and descended upon Vancouver, BC. Canadians love their skyscrapers and their cities, by comparison to America's, are incredibly clean. It was here that I got an electrifying career jolt and was imbued with the notion that perhaps a city could be a great place to live. We visited Simon Fraser University, centrally located Stanley Park, Butchart Gardens, and, of utmost importance to all college students, the bar-riddled gaslight district. Vancouver enjoys the benefit of being wonderfully sited as it sits in a natural bowl surrounded by water with five thousand-foot mountain ranges as a backdrop. It was certainly a sight to see and it left a marked positive impression on me, which was reaffirmed when I visited it again when it hosted the 1986 World's Fair. This was especially true when you consider the city I was forced to return to.

After surviving Washington State, which is somewhat akin to saying, "after surviving England's Victorian period," I returned to my tiny hometown in western New York in the spring of 1974. At warp speed, I became impregnated with the numbing reality that there wasn't a job market for designers in a factory town. By career necessity it was inevitable that I would wind up in Buffalo and it should be said that Buffalo taught me some hard lessons concerning mankind's worshiping of stupidity and greed. It was a dying city. The freeway had cut out her heart, and downtown was an isolated strip of rundown buildings of undeterminable future in light of a worsening economy and the closing of the steel mills in the surrounding suburbs. No one was talking proud back then.

Nevertheless, I indulged in her rampant bar life on Elmwood Avenue, visited the Albright Knox Art Gallery frequently, and eventually wound up living in an architect's home just outside La Fayette Circle on Richmond Avenue, which was one of five radial avenues that sliced through Buffalo at odd angles, adding some semblance of flair and interest. Buffalo, you see, was designed by Frenchmen Pierre Charles L'Enfant, one of the precursors to the profession of landscape architecture. L'Enfant also designed Washington, Detroit, and Indianapolis on the radial axis so familiar to his beloved Paris. Ever an emotional man, he died in the streets of Washington complaining that he was never understood. In death he left a curse upon future landscape architects, in particular me, that they likewise would never be understood. While not personally understood, I began to understand cities: what made them great or mediocre and what could possibly make them magnificent. I felt somewhat headily intellectual with this acquired knowledge, but then, lose all hope ye who enter here, I moved to Phoenix.

Phoenix was the epitome of stupidity and greed, which is as good an explanation as any as to what attracted me to her. After a stint of utterly uninspiring jobs with a series of landscape contractors, I finally hooked on with a position as a landscape-architect-in-training with the largest architectural firm in the state. As one would say in my tiny western New York hometown—my shit was hot.

From whence came Phoenix? A metropolis located smack

dab in the middle of the Sonoran desert, where it certainly didn't belong. The freeway dominated the city. Big time developers fought over the location of her business center resulting in the formation of two downtowns with neither a strong contender for architectural greatness. Things were worse on the outskirts, as light industrial park upon light industrial park sprang up and were immediately engulfed by sprawling suburbs. I became embroiled in a battle, which I eloquently embellish in my autobiography, *Career in Crisis*, which appears destined never to be published; that being the battle between the greens and the grays. The greens (my firm included) saw Phoenix as an oasis amidst a sea of ugly, useless desert while the grays championed the use of indigenous plant materials as a means of saving water and a way of mirroring the surrounding greater environment. The grays eventually won, but not without battle scars. Some parts of Phoenix are incongruent, going from one lot green, one lot gray, with no apparent rhyme or reason. The city was growing faster than any urban planner could figure out what it was that she needed most. Cheap out-of-town developers, most from exclusive Orange County, California readily promoted schlock they wouldn't accept in their own backyards. Rapidly written and revised zoning ordinances couldn't save her as development raged out of control.

Quite simply, Phoenix became a mish-mashed mess. It's only fitting that this was the town in which I decided to carve out a career. I performed attractive if not exceptional design work that became lost in the maze of the cheap, shoddy, quick buck, get-in-and-get-out design hell I was living in. I took refuge by delving into regular weekend trips to San Diego during Phoenix's oppressive summers.

San Diego. Oh San Diego! A city with much of the same

problems as Phoenix but blessed with the location and climate to bail her out. She also had a strong sense of Spanish Mission history on her side. The dredging of swampland to form Mission Bay, never popular with hard line environmentalists, was the impetus to a flourishing tourism economy. The downtown gaslight district, Old Town, Mission Beach, Balboa Park, Coronado Island, filthy wealthy, yet squeaky clean La Jolla. San Diego is a city of hustle and bustle with a beauty to match Vancouver and a nightlife to rival New Orleans. With such a jewel shimmering in front of my wandering eyes is it any wonder I would relocate to Palm Springs?

I really didn't have a choice as I had worn out my welcome in Phoenix and had to get out of town fast. Fleeing to Palm Desert, which lies thirteen miles east of the Coachella Valley's flagship city of Palm Springs set in the heart of the searing Colorado Desert, I landed a job with a high-end custom residential landscape architect and settled into becoming a tool of the rich. Here it became painfully obvious to me that ten percent of the US population hoarded ninety percent of the wealth and that I definitely didn't fall into that ten percent.

Traveling the Coachella Valley from west to east there occurs historic Palm Springs, middle class Cathedral City, upper class and somewhat uppity Rancho Mirage, middle management infested worker bee Palm Desert, stratospherically upper class and somewhat hermitic Indian Wells, wealthy come lately La Quinta, working class Indio, and lower class but on the economic rise Coachella.

Agriculture defined the early years, then tourism crept in, then golf took over. The Coachella Valley is a golf mecca, with more courses per square mile than any other area in the world. This shocks the water conscience, who repeatedly warn that the well will run dry and royally pisses off the golfers who are distracted by such noise.

The cities themselves could fittingly be compared to the constantly warring countries of the Middle East. They are not much united on anything and each is convinced that the other has given it a raw deal, the short end of the stick, or incited border-related logistical problems much the same as when Israel moved in. So rather than taking a regional planning approach, these city states have decided to become little empires unto themselves.

Palm Springs has a recognizable downtown core with an active thriving nightlife, so the community does have something to work with. Developers eye the foothills to the San Jacinto mountain range as a place to build huge homes for retired couples reflecting great wealth and a whole-hearted belief in a value system that prompted Steely Dan's "The Royal Scam." The Aqua Caliente band of Cahuilla Indians possess alternating 640-acre sections of land, which they lease to commercial real estate interests who refer to the ground as the, "golden checkerboard." All in all, Palm Springs still has promise.

Cathedral City was a repository for the suburban middle class ideal and its subsequent cracker box houses all in a row. The city hired professional planners to make it look grand. They shot for the moon with a Spanish Revival-meets-Art Deco civic complex and the whole city turned gaudy as a result.

Rancho Mirage has no recognizable downtown core but boasts of a "restaurant district" on banners along the highway. Most of them close up by ten o'clock so nightlife never spills over into civil unrest.

Palm Desert is a city that tries harder and is a virtual haven for women aspiring to the status of Stepford Wives. It boasts El Paseo, a rich shopping district, which locals say rivals Rodeo Drive in Beverly Hills. I wouldn't know because I couldn't afford to shop there or at the other there. Its planning department is populated by design "experts" who hold professional registrations in absolutely nothing and make my life a living hell. There's an Art in Public Places program and The Living Desert regional wildlife park that are kind of nice. In terms of actually becoming a midsize, big league city, Palm Desert will have to try even harder because she now ranks number two.

Indian Wells strives to not look like a city and has pulled it off. You can drive through it on the main drag and not notice much except sidewalks and landscaping and no noticeable character. Per capita, it's the wealthiest community in the United States and an apparent city-wide fear of robbery keeps the residents hidden in their houses or detained behind exclusive country club walls. There are no schools and children are seen for the rabble rousing little bastards that they are. This would explain an incident at the local food store where the police were called in to remove green clad little heathens selling Girl Scout cookies and disturbing the peace. The unpressed charge, of course, was loitering.

La Quinta is now getting a little big for its britches. City fathers want to renovate "old town" even if it never existed in the past. At least this will create some form and sense of a downtown, but old? Give me a break. It does host an annual arts festival that is gaining in notoriety while allowing residents to feel cultured.

Indio is hopeless. Its planners are rudderless. There's an identity crisis between the lower, hard working middle class that is and what politicians want them to be.

Coachella has the best chance to quickly become an actual city. There isn't much in her way. There's a recognizable downtown core that could be upgraded to reflect the festive atmosphere of her predominate rabidly hard working, phobically Roman Catholic Mexican population. Ignoring the obvious, the planning department wants to create an "entertainment district" in another part of town featuring three high-end resort/golf course communities, thus creating a solid new tax base and lining city coffers. When I was included among the planning firms that interviewed for the glorious design contract I asked, "What will become of the people who are already here?" Eechee-Iyah-I-yi-yi—they didn't know. But I knew. They would be pushed out, as they always are in the name of progress, once again paying homage to "The Royal Scam."

Good God! What a conglomeration of vanity and avarice. Unfortunately, unlike the Middle East, they can't bomb each other out so we could start over even though this is sorely needed. As if by some unstoppable force of economic nature the rich get richer while the poor flee, urgently searching for an affordable place to live. They travel due south along the western shores of the Salton Sea into the long waiting arms of long forgotten Salton City. More on this later.

So while not an international or even a national jet setter, one can see I've seen my share of cities. What I have observed and learned is this: cities are like fingerprints—every one is different. Yet, in function, every one is remarkably alike. Herein lies the crux of urban planning, which is to accommodate a certain commonality of purpose yet establish a character and identity all its own.

Historically, identity was the last thing on city dwellers' minds. Safety in numbers was the driving force in their formation. Once within close proximity to each other, craftsmen adept at various trades discovered that battering for goods and services led to a better lifestyle. Soon nasty little problems like sewage disposal and resulting plagues popped up, but in actuality, these helped to regulate problems associated with overcrowding. So, for the most part, cities benefited mankind and the fast rising notion of civilization.

Cities were sited along waterways for convenience of travel and trade, on level plains for access to farming tracts, on hillsides for surveillance and defense, and just about anywhere else man could obtain a foothold and then a stronghold against the forces of nature and enemy tribes.

Lewis Mumford is recognized as the quintessential authority on cities. His classic *The City in History* won the National Book Award in 1962. Mumford's work is an exhaustive (576 page) look at the formative history and eventual logistical problems of cities. He viewed them as centers of culture and a setting in which heroic architecture could rise up to define the aspirations of mankind trying to separate itself from the ravages of the wild. Most of all, he saw cities as places where mankind congregated its aggregate knowledge to advance the cause of civilization.

Cities became great because the collective personality and common belief systems of their populations made them that way. They represented the common efforts of mankind to rise to the status of the most intelligent and dominant species on earth. Late in his ninety-five year life, Mumford became preoccupied with the destructiveness of nuclear war. Perhaps he was moved by the obliteration of Hiroshima and Nakasaki, two of Japan's largest and oldest cities, at the end of World War II. It must have rattled Mumford to see that cities, once the ultimate embodiment of civilization, could be so easily disposed of. What did this say of mankind? While it took generations to create the great architecture of cities, or even great cities themselves, they could be destroyed in seconds. This did not bode well for mankind.

Hot on the heels of Mumford's manifesto, along came Lawrence Halprin, a man destined to become a giant in the field of landscape architecture, with his offering, *Cities*. Halprin firmly believed cities fostered and drove human creativity to its highest level. He broke cities down to their most basic elements—surfaces, water, and trees—but stressed that cities were more, much more to a man married to a professional ballerina dancer whom he danced with on the rooftop of his office building during his lunch breaks. Halprin instinctively knew that cities had a choreography and a life, for if they didn't, what was the point of inhabiting them?

Garret Eckbo wrote passionately that the automobile would slice apart the urban fabric, leaving ugliness and lost neighborhoods in its wake. No one listened.

James Howard Kunstler echoed Eckbo's concern two decades later in *The Geography of Nowhere*. He, more than any other author, most firmly placed his finger upon the pulse of what made cities great, and conversely, why most of them weren't anymore. The automobile was certainly public enemy number one, but it was more than that. Initially cities had a core area, usually the seats of government, entertainment and sports arenas, areas used for gatherings or public forums, then shops, then homes. Everything was within walking distance because, believe it or not, people walked prior to 1900. American cities adopted the square, with church on one side of the park and city hall on the other. Shops lined the flanking sides, sometimes with homes above the shops, and other houses in close proximity. These were true neighborhoods. *Again, everything was within walking distance.*

More than the automobile what, to date, has changed the face and complexion of cities the most have been zoning ordinances based more on the perceived virtues of order rather than the historic dictates of comfort, so comfortable in fact, that early cities radiated a sense of place. Subliminally, people in a neighborhood relied on each other, knew one another, and looked out for each other. Zoning ordinances changed all that. Schools over here, factories over there, offices in the commercial areas, bars away from homes and children, city hall downtown, hospitals uptown; everything miles and miles apart and only conventionally reachable by automobile. This wasn't a vibrant urban fabric woven for human comfort, it was a patchwork quilt lacking the thread to draw it together because roadways replaced thread and separated everything into sterile little squares. Zoning ordinances born of a need to create order and harmony actually begat chaos and estrangement. Neighborhoods fell apart. Once this happened, the door swung wide open for the worst of the worst and the suburbs were born. The creeping crud of suburbia mushroomed like a nuclear blast out from the city centers and swallowed up the rural hinterlands of America much like a school of piranhas swallows up horseflesh.

The blind ambition of zoning ordinances continued to wreak havoc as each successive layer of order led to a vast homogenization of similar uses in similar spaces, which opened and closed at similar times. Cities and towns that were once vibrant places to the point where something spontaneous and unpredictable might actually happen there were now turned into places where the predictable always ruled and people were too bored to question why. If cities are once again to be vibrant, then diversity or *mixed-use* has to come back into being. You see, cities and ecology are in one way remarkably similar: diversity always leads to the better health of the system. Less diversity equates to less health. It's not rocket science.

As much as nature was expelled from early cities, once man let down his guard, she crept back in, infiltrating at the edges or introduced as parks, open space, street trees. Man feels comfortable when he can control nature and when doing so oftentimes comes to the realization that he misses nature when it's not around. Eventually most city denizens came to realize that there wasn't enough nature in their midst and developed a deep appreciation for anything that reminded them of it. A city dweller's relationship with nature is like a teenager being picked up by his mother after a high school dance. Although he completely tries to ignore her he knows that he needs her.

Perhaps because they have so little of it, urbanites seem to be drawn to nature, either outwardly or subliminally. They have a deep appreciation for street trees. Movies such as *Autumn in New York* highlight the civic pride inhabitants have in their limited natural surroundings. Marie Wynn's *Red-Tails In Love*, the story of a young male red-tail hawk that set up shop in the heart of New York City on a luxury residential high-rise tower adjacent to famed Central Park, captured local, then national, and eventually world-wide attention. The hawk, named Pale Male, and his third mate later appeared on the March/April cover of *Audubon* magazine in an article that documented the breadth of public outcry when real estate developer Richard Cohen and CNN news personality Paula Zahn evicted the birds by having their nest destroyed because it blocked the multimillion dollar view from their picture window, and to be fair to the humans, they grew tired of dried bird poop and dead prey, mostly pigeons, littering their window ledge. Outraged New Yorkers, most notably actress Mary Tyler Moore, came to the aid of the hawks, and an ardent group of protestors kept a three-week long vigil from across the street. Author Marie Wynn donned a red cardinal suit because hawk suits were unavailable (on such short notice). Signs such as, "Honk 4 Hawks" were hoisted up toward passing motorists, who honked with gusto as everyone else basically raised holy hell. When a special, cleaner stainless steel nest holder was designed by architect Dan Ionescu, Cohen relented to pressure and the birds returned home.

Almost missed in all the civic anarchy was the fact that this wasn't the first time Pale Male had been given the boot. The raptor had been nesting at the site since 1993 and he and various mates had fledged twenty-three offspring. In the same year ('93) that Pale Male's first nest was removed, Wynn and other Audubon members enlisted the aid of the US Fish and Wildlife Service, who cited the Migratory Bird Treaty Act of 1918 as grounds to threaten a lawsuit against the building's inhabitants if they did not allow Pale Male and his mate to fly free and build their nest wherever they chose. Recent bureaucratic tampering with the act had, in fact, allowed Cohen to remove the birds in 2004. Why was it necessary to modify the original language of the act? Will it be restored to its original form? Government officials and staff just can't leave well enough alone. While Pale Male and his current mate Lola indeed enjoy the privileges of media darlings, other birds in other areas have been compromised.

In the grand scheme of things, what does it matter if just two birds do or don't inhabit the ledge of a high-rise building in the most urban city on earth in their new nest precariously tethered to pigeon spikes and existing on nothing more than (pardon the pun) a wing and a prayer? In some ways it matters more than Yellowstone National Park or the San Diego Zoo. While these two places represent magnificent preservation and restoration efforts for the benefit of nature, seventy percent of New York City residents will never visit these facilities. Pale Male and Lola, on the other hand, and the media frenzy they engendered, reminded New Yorkers that nature is resilient, and in a live and let live atmosphere, it and mankind can find ways to coexist. On another level the issue is more subliminal than that. Wilderness touches our soul and somehow causes us to realize our place in the universe. It wipes away the layer of self-absorption that mankind uses as the shield to destroy nature in the first place in the name of progress, in the name of highest and best use of the land, in the name of anything we can think of that lets us go ahead and do what we wish to do anyways with no concern for the consequences to the "lower species."

This is why a tree in the city is worth its weight in gold, why people ignore the rolling eyes of hard core environmentalists and put out bird feeders, why potted geraniums appear on the fire escapes of apartments in the worst parts of Harlem. Why, on some subliminal level, mankind inherently connects to some tiny part of nature.

So what has been learned about restoring cities and suburbs? First, that the automobile must be held in check and eventually eliminated. Secondly, the more nature that can be introduced, the better. In order for cities to have a life, life must be all around—human and otherwise. Third, that ill-conceived and utterly repressive zoning ordinances worshiped by governmental planners of questionable ability have to be overthrown, ransacked, and burned.

In order for cities to be great places they need great spaces, and above all, these spaces must be within walking distance. But if cities aren't attractive or, better yet, compellingly aesthetic, it will be a very dull and dreary walk—day after day, week after week, year after year. Who but a sadist wants this? Fortunately there are some things that we can easily do. These are:

- Identify and reinforce the city's purpose/function.
- Push the automobile out of city centers.
- Introduce mass transit.
- Unify the building facade(s).
- Improve the graphic signage/wayfinding system.
- Protect and then enhance the surrounding natural terrain.
- Reintroduce nature.
- Give visitors a reason to stay.

Most citizens of any given city don't know the original or ongoing reasons why the place exists. While Boston and parts of Philadelphia exude history, Detroit and Phoenix are hard put to visually or subliminally tell the citizenry what their history is. Any city with an identity crisis is a city destined for sprawl because there is no anchor, no magnet, nothing to encourage planned *concentric growth* away from the center.

Some cities lose or switch their purpose. Kansas City was a Midwestern cattle industry rail town. When the country went to trucking, she declined. By reinforcing the visual drama of her downtown architectural elements by taking advantage of a serendipitous knoll-like setting, she became the vertical beacon of the plains, drawing approving attention and eliciting anticipation from miles away.

Buffalo was a Great Lakes port city whose base economy

was further enhanced by the building of the Erie Canal. When railroads replaced canals as the fastest viable means of shipping, Buffalo declined. Her middle class suburbs turned to working in the rapidly expanding steel mill trade as a means of survival. Ditto for Pittsburgh. Only by diversifying their economies and promoting innovative urban renewal programs did these cities rise again.

Whatever a city's current reason for being, its character should immediately make that obvious.

The car has dissected city centers and isolated neighborhoods into floating urban islands of dissimilar functions. Now some cities are fighting back by deciding to charge drivers for penetrating their core with nuisance automobiles, thus encouraging mass transit, bicycling, and walking. These cities were fast to learn they were better off for it. Cars are unsafe to pedestrians while the roadways they must travel on chew up land where land is most at a premium. By pushing the automobile further and further away from the center, safety is increased, air pollution lessened, and land freed up for numerous other human purposes. A lack of automobiles lining the streets visually creates a sense of more open space and relief from congestion.

People have to get into the city centers, of course, and mass transit, be it a bus system, light rail, or ferries, must accommodate this.

When mass transit replaces cars, less natural resources (steel, petroleum based plastics, synthetic rubber, etc.) are used and fuel efficiency on a rider-per-mile-traveled basis is dramatically increased.

Older cities usually have an architectural character owing to the fact that at least some of their original buildings were left intact. Yesterday's building systems, which depended on the limitations of available materials and construction methods, were different from today's. Steel and plastic have changed all this. Today, several city centers are a mismatched mix of architectural styles. While variety is the spice of life, in architecture, it can be the seed of chaos. A unified street front architectural facade enhances the street scene and reinforces a sense of place. Whether leaning toward the old or the new, there should be an almost rhythmic harmony that blurs transitions between buildings and connects the built environment.

Starting in the mid-seventies, urban planners became concerned that cities were being overwhelmed with signage. Typically, they turned to their zoning ordinances for a solution. The new ordinances restricted square footages, colors, length of messages, materials, and just about anything else that would inspire creativity. By the nineties it was generally recognized that sign ordinances weren't facilitating the original intent of signage blending into and enhancing the street scene and the concept of "wayfinding" come to the fore. The essence of signage is that it should enable the reader to assimilate minimal information that will allow her/him to find their way to a destination. Signage should never (although it frequently is) be confused with advertising, which belongs in magazines and on television and not on buildings. Wayfinding is a physical or graphic system that, through either shape, form, color, wording and mapping, or material selection, leads the follower to the intended destination. Disney is a master at the technique. The key to pedestrian wayfinding systems is that they be of *human scale*. This makes the system friendly and helpful as opposed to belittling and domineering.

While cities must have a recognizable center to establish their identities, it must be remembered that this center is merely the hub of a far greater community expanding outward in scale to a region. In *Nature-Friendly Communities*, Christopher Duerksen and Cara Snyder champion land conservation and habitat restoration, providing nineteen case studies from across America. In design school I was taught to conceptually think big, then little, and that the details would take care of themselves. Pursuant to this, an open space/habitat restoration plan is best served if it starts with an overall region and then more sharply focuses through rural areas on into the city center. Today, the problem is that with increasing frequency large government entities from the national, state, and county levels are turning their backs on wildlife preservation by relaxing regulations and cutting or eliminating sources of funding. While hard core environmentalists are quick to point out that this is simply a manifestation of Bush's war against the environment being carried out by the rank and file, it should be noted that this is also the fate of social programs. Politicians are adept at finger pointing. States say they are hogtied by the feds. Counties point to the state and then the national government as the reason why they accomplish virtually nothing of lasting value. Cities point to the county, which, of course, points back and says, "Patient, heal thyself." And so, in terms of environmental restoration, the individual citizen must. If it's going to be, it's up to me. Local grassroots organizations are going to have to accept the task of fighting big government in the guerilla warfare of habitat restoration, limiting sprawl, and overturning zoning ordinances that are well-intentioned but meaningless.

Zoning ordinances invariably attack what they perceive to see as the evils of development in the area of limiting density, all the while failing to notice the basic fact that density, when it's done right, leaves more open space. Dear Lord, what will it take to drive this point home into the collective consciousness of politicians and planners? We have been trying for thirty-five years and most of them still don't get it. But on the local citizen action level, they are starting to.

Related to habitat and open space preservation is the issue of urban infill, which is a problem common to ill-planned, fast growing southwestern cities. In an effort to escape escalating land costs, developers employed the process of "leap frogging," whereby they acquired lower cost land further away from developed land, developed it, and literally forced buyers to clamor for the cities to extend infrastructure out to them in an appeasement response to charging higher property taxes. The land that was "leap frogged" over often sat vacant for years, degenerating into weed infested lots and community eyesores. Again, the only way to prevent this is to change the language and intent of zoning ordinances, and some cities are finally starting to do this. The vacant infill lots often offer up the opportunity to provide parks and green space, but they will never be able to become as ecologically diverse as the land on the outskirts of town that the developers are in a frenzy to gobble up and environmentalists seek to preserve. Some responsible developers are now coming back into the cities and building on infill lots. It's more expensive, access isn't as good, profitability suffers, but the city is better off.

In previous books and papers I've championed mini-wildlife parks and preserves in city centers, often on the aforementioned infill land. Now, upon reading *A Different Nature: The Paradoxical World of Zoos and Their Uncertain Future* by David Hancocks, I am reassessing whether this could ever really happen. Habitat is the essential issue. Creatures need a lot of it and most of the world's existing zoos don't even have enough space.

Hancocks cites the marvelous Sonora Desert Museum

outside of Tucson, Arizona as a fine example of a regionally oriented facility representing a specific biome and suggests that this is a more useful and practical way to go in the future. In the same vein, the American Society of Landscape Architects has been promoting separate short grass prairie and tall grass prairie preserve facilities for the last ten years. Most of the world's big city zoos try too hard to be all things to all wildlife observers, often to the detriment of the animals.

New thought not only revolves around realistic looking enclosures, but also recognizes that the well-being and comfort of the wild animals should be placed ahead of that of the human viewers. This necessitates providing places to hide and opportunities for the creatures to view large sweeping vistas in a fashion similar to the freedom they would enjoy in their natural terrain.

A regional facility, while not as likely as big zoos to gross huge sums of money, can zero in on specific lessons inherent to a specific area. The Arizona Sonoran Desert Museum's initial purpose was to encourage Tucson residents to take a cue from their surrounding environment and landscape their houses with drought tolerant indigenous plant material. The facility literally turned the fortunes of Tucson around, as it now stands as one of the most ecologically in-tune cities in the world.

The greatest task for future urban planners is to identify and examine what makes cities memorable. *What would give visitors a reason to stay?* Tourism dollars can account for up to forty percent of any given city's economy. Innovative to heroic architecture, lively street scenes, festive nightlife, street trees and other greenery, and a sense of place all come to mind. What's important to note is that the megatrends of fossil fuel depletion, increasingly more difficult water purification, and escalating levels of sewage treatment dictate that at least ninety percent of the entire world's population will live in cities before the turn of the twenty-second century. If you don't believe me, read James Howard Kuntsler's recently published (2005) *The Long Emergency: Surviving the Converging Catastrophes of the Twenty-First Century.* It will literally make the hair stand up on the back of your neck.

With the coming human stampede back to the cities, is it any wonder that urban planners are now hard put to devise renaturalization and restoration methodologies that will not only make cities accommodating, but in the final analysis, great?

Chapter Eight: Quotes
Heightening Public Environmental Awareness

When in the course of human Events, it becomes necessary for one People to dissolve the Political Bands which have connected them with another, and to assume among the Powers of the Earth, the separate and equal Station to which the Laws of Nature and of Nature's God entitle them, a decent Respect to the Opinions of Mankind requires that they should declare the causes which impel them to the Separation.

We hold these truths to be self-evident, that all Men are created equal, that they are endowed by their Creator with certain unalienable Rights, that among these are Life, Liberty, and the Pursuit of Happiness — That to secure these Rights, Governments are instituted among Men, deriving their just Powers from the Consent of the Governed, that whenever any Form of Government becomes destructive of these Ends, it is the Right of the People to alter or to abolish it, and to institute new Government, laying its Foundation on such Principles, and organizing its Powers in such Form, as to them shall seem most likely to effect their Safety and Happiness . . .[33]

The Declaration of Independence
Action of Second Continental Congress
July 4th, 1776

The front line in the battle to save the American environment is occupied by ordinary people taking on extraordinary odds to defend those communities.[34]

The Riverkeepers
John Cronin and Robert F. Kennedy, Jr.

New groups, new concerns, and new strategies may still fulfill the prediction of some historians that American environmentalism will one day be regarded as the most significant social and political movement of the century.[35]

Losing Ground
Mark Dowie

When The War Against the Greens *first appeared in the spring of 1994, there was a widespread media perception that the environmental movement had pretty much peaked with the mass rallies of Earth Day 1990, and that environmental regulation was now hurting the American economy.*

Despite polls showing that 76 percent of Americans considered themselves green, the New York Times *environmental reporter was promoting the Wise Use/Property Rights backlash as "the third wave" of environmentalism.*

"I think that the (Wise Use) movement is maybe one of the most important and interesting movements to arise in environmentalism in a long time," he claimed, "because they are prying into the environmental issues that we've all grappled with for two decades. Is there really global warming? Is there really an ozone problem? Does toxic waste cleanup really represent the best use of public financing?" He went on to portray the anti-enviro backlash as a bottom-up citizen movement. "The Property Rights groups I know have no corporate funding at all. They're mom-and-pop community environmental groups," he claimed, and, because he was from the New York Times, *other reporters believed him.*

ABC's Nightline *reported, "For a lot of people in this country, the environmental movement has gone too far. What's more, they're organizing into a powerful nationwide coalition (called Wise Use), and their battle cry is, "The environmental movement has become an environmental disaster."*

In going for the counterintuitive story of a citizen uprising against what then Texas pest exterminator—now House majority leader—Tom DeLay called "the jackbooted EPA Gestapo," the mainstream media failed to do their own investigative reporting. Rather they acted as a transmission belt for more conservative media outlets.[36]

War Against the Greens
David Helvarg

Chapter Eight

Heightening Public Environmental Awareness

How wimpy and utterly pathetic did it seem when the decade of the nineties, the supposed "green decade," drew to a close leaving no significant social or environmental upheaval in its wake and causing environmentalists to wonder, "Are we going to revolt or what?"

When our founding fathers signed the Declaration of Independence, basically telling King George III of Britain that they weren't going to eat his crap anymore, the die was cast. There could be no turning back or do-overs. It was freedom or bust. While fifty-six signatures appear at the end of the document, a committee of five men was appointed to draft the work and these five men mainly relied on one, Thomas Jefferson, to do the bulk of the writing. Jefferson drew from the theory of Natural Law postulated by Swiss legal philosopher Emerich de Vattal, which upheld that unrelenting civic virtue ultimately led to the pursuit of happiness. Concern for the natural world, unfortunately, was not what was meant by the "Laws of Nature" and "Nature's God" as the terms appear in the document. The twenty-first century's laws of nature that provide the reason as to why the planet's health is declining didn't even cross Jefferson's mind way back then.

Jefferson and his contemporaries, George Washington, John Adams, James Madison, and beloved Benjamin Franklin, lived in a world quite unlike that of their nemesis the British Empire. Four-fifths of the landmass that would become the continental United States was uninhabited and unexploited of its natural resources. One could only imagine what natural riches lay beyond the boundaries of the frontier, which, at that time, would constitute the eastern borders of Ohio, Kentucky, Tennessee, and Alabama.

Jefferson envisioned and supported an agrarian society and isolation from the constantly warring nations of Europe. Perhaps he gained a distaste for French politics and the extravagant monarchy of Louis XVI when he served as minister (ambassador) to France from 1784 to 1789. An adroit man and skilled statesman, Jefferson, no doubt, was cognizant of the mounting grumblings of the French peasantry that was the precursor to the French Revolution, perhaps the bloodiest citizen revolt in history. As he checked out of France in 1789, the revolution checked in. Americans would be safer in America. This and the fact that, by now, new French dictator Napoleon Bonaparte desperately needed money to finance his faltering conquest of Western Europe led to his consummation of the Louisiana Purchase in 1803 as the climatic event to his first term as president and the subsequent Lewis and Clark Expedition of 1804–1806.

In actuality, the Lewis and Clark Expedition had been planned prior to the Louisiana Purchase. President Jefferson had long believed in and dreamed of a river passage, a "Northwest Passage" that would open up America to settlement and commerce on the western frontier. When Jefferson got the news in late 1806 that such didn't exist, he was not too particularly despondent. The land that had been explored contained vast stores of fresh water, fertile soil, timber, and game. America had certainly still gotten a bargain that he would long be remembered for.

What he is most remembered for, however, is his true intellect. He, Madison, and Franklin, the architects of the American Revolution, were haunted by accounts of the rapidly developing French Revolution. Thus, it could be argued that revolutions shaped their thinking as much as their thinking shaped history. Which brings us to the Green Revolution. Although this title was initially given to the technological expansion of agriculture, it faded in the fifties. It was taken over by the counterculture of the sixties and now refers to environmental causes great and small. Red, white, blue, or green, the American Environmental Revolution is long overdue. Here are the reasons why.

Let's return to the preamble of the Declaration of Independence and the so stated basic three rights—Life, Liberty, and the Pursuit of Happiness.

Our lives are daily threatened by toxins, pollutants, and/or a surplus of new "designer drugs" held out to Americans as good for them by corporations who have historically proven that they couldn't care less about our well-being. Only our prowess as producers and consumers much matters to them while they scheme on ways to outsource jobs, eliminate worker benefits, and rob middle-management of its pensions a few short years before they come due.

Life. What life? The corporations have once again risen to the status of demigods that they possessed at the turn of the twentieth century when Carnegie, Rockefeller, Morgan, and Ford ruled the roost. Without Teddy Roosevelt the general American populace would have become little more than underpaid indentured servants to their omnipotent employers. Today, without Teddy Roosevelt (because he died), the corporations have taken a circuitous route back to the glory years of their predecessors. Computers threaten to steal our identity while the agricultural byproducts of genetic engineering threaten to produce new species at no known cost to the environment. Make no mistake about it, corporations threaten to run and ruin our lives, while all the while we find it difficult to believe that we can turn to the government for protection as they look and function the same as the corporations look and function. Have Americans lost contact with their leaders? Do our leaders know who we are and what we want? In a medically dominated society that elongates life, is there any plan that makes the added years worth the living?

Liberty. What liberty? Sure we are free, or so we tell ourselves. We cannot liberate ourselves from the effects of despoiled air and water, from contaminants in our food supplies, from a rising cancer rate, from birth deformities and child autism. We are at liberty to see our children live less well than we did while our parents know that we live less well then they did. Why does our quality of life seem stuck in a downward spiral? And what can reverse this trend? Yes, we have liberty, but what do we do with it? Why have Americans grown complacent to worsening environmental conditions? Do we not see the injustices that abound about us? Or is the problem that we feel completely powerless to do anything about them? What kind of liberty is that?

Pursuit of happiness. What pursuit of happiness? Most of us have given up on happy and will settle for comfortable and content. Overwhelmed by the numbing insignificance of an existence amidst the churning juggernauts of big government fueled by big business, we have simply given up on making any form of an individual difference. We are cogs in a thundering, piston-pounding machine that is racing out of control and shortly destined to run out of gas. The historic formula for the pursuit of happiness among mankind and among the "lower species" has been to perpetuate its given species, extend a genetic code, buy time, and see what evolves. Hope and pray that whatever evolves gets a handle on this pursuit of happiness thing because we sure the hell didn't.

So with our God-given rights to life, liberty, and the pursuit of happiness definitely compromised, primarily by a government of our own making, what can we do? Again readers, one and all, and in deafening unison, let's reiterate the most enlightening words in the Declaration of Independence: *That when any Form of Government becomes destructive to these ends, it is* the Right of the People to alter or abolish it, *and to institute new Government . . .* So precedent has been set. The people did it before and they can do it again. There is only one solution to meet the cancer of the worsening environmental crisis head on. Revolt! Revolt! Revolt!

The problem with political revolutions is that they are extremely bloody. Death defines them. Human sacrifice is lifted up to the cause. Why must it be this way? To prove that enough is enough, and that fire will be met with fire, the backlash to injustice is usually steeped in enough conviction to risk life and limb to eliminate it. Why must it be this way? Monarchs, tyrants, and dictators are single-minded and hardheaded. Their primary goals are first to stay in power, and second, to live extravagantly off the sweat of the brows of their subjects. Why must it be this way? American government is not a monarchy or a dictatorship. It was, in fact, designed in such a manner to prevent a totalitarian state from ever forming, which brings us to the formation of our government, under the dictates of one of the most fair-minded documents among mankind—the Constitution of the United States of America. Reading it is to appreciate the genius and forethought of our founding fathers. Comprehending its intent causes one to look at government as it exists today and ask, where did we go wrong and why must it be this way?

While the Constitution is rife with Jeffersonian ideals, the man himself was not a signer of the great work. He was in France witnessing the decadence of Louis the XVI's court and most likely wondering just how much stuff Marie Antoinette could cram atop her head. The drafting of the Constitution fell to a quiet, unassuming, slight little man who deserves to receive more credit for the intellectual giant that he was.

James Madison, the fourth president of the United States, was a diminutive man who stood five feet, four inches tall and weighed one hundred pounds. A Virginian and a contemporary in thought and vision with Jefferson, he favored a strong central government versus a loose confederation of states. The strength of the document he crafted is reflected in the creation of three branches of government: executive, legislative, and judicial—the President, Congress (House of Representatives and the Senate), and the Supreme Court. While the presidential post was to be viewed as the effective leadership of the country, he could not operate independent of Congress. The primary function of the Supreme Court was to provide ongoing interpretation of the Constitution as the supreme law of the land. And, Tom Delay be damned, the Supreme Court is set up to operate in anonymity from the other two branches of government and the population of the country at large. With this being the case, the Supreme Court is designed to be *incorruptible.*

The pure genius of the Constitution is manifested in the establishment of Congressional bodies that would function independently in decision-making matters, which virtually assured that there would be a system of checks and balances internal to the operation of the country. Each state would have two senators and its population would determine its number of congressmen (or women) at the rate of one representative per every twenty thousand inhabitants.

While Jefferson smiled on the formation and ratification of the Constitution, he worried that it would be ineffective without a Bill of Rights, a fact that he intimidated to Madison in their correspondences. Jefferson wrote from France: "I will add what I do not like. First, the omission of a bill of rights providing clearly, and without the aid of sophisms for freedom of religion, freedom of the press, protection against standing armies, restriction against monopolies, the eternal & unremitting force of the habeas corpus laws, and trials by jury in all matters of fact, tried by the laws of the land & not by the laws of nations."

The Bill of Rights was attached to the Constitution as its first ten amendments in 1791, during George Washington's first term as the first president of the United States. Through the years, seventeen more amendments were added, for a total of twenty-seven (effectively twenty-six as the 18th Amendment, Prohibition, was later repealed). What's important for environmentalists to note is that their best chance for lasting environmental justice lies in obtaining an amendment to the Constitution. In the absence of this, the first amendment will have to do. It states: *Congress shall make no law respecting an establishment of religion, or prohibiting the free exercise thereof; or abridging the freedom of speech, or of the press; or the right of the people peaceably to assemble, and to petition the government for a redress of grievances.*

Petition the Government for a redress of grievances. How

does one or a body of people go about doing that? I was somewhat surprised that the attorney from Earthjustice (800-584-6460, earthjustice.org) returned my call within a half-hour's time. No, he told me, I was not the first person to have this "amendment to the Constitution" idea. He didn't feel that an amendment was really necessary as the framework of the Constitution had ample references that would allow interpretation on the environment's behalf. Besides that, it was his considered opinion that there were plenty of other perfectly good laws on the books, "If people only respected them." I stated that, although not an attorney, it seemed to me that many of the amendments seemed to either reword or restate what was implied in the main framework of the Constitution as clarifications. Because of this, the proposed environmental amendment should have some precedent. "Not the way to go," he felt.

I stated that I always thought the US government had sovereign immunity and was therefore impossible to sue. Not true, he assured me. The government is sued all the time. Not the White House per se, but suits are leveled in federal courts against its various agencies—the Environmental Protection Agency and the US Forest Service, to name but a few. The tactic was to entice these federal courts into hearing a specific petition or appeal that either interested or shocked the judge(s).

He went on to say that Earthjustice's approach was on the international level through the United Nations. They were working to form international environmental treaties—check out their web site, which I did.

I didn't print out the ninety-two page document because their brief summation suits my purposes. It reads:

Earthjustice uses US courts and international tribunals to hold corporations and governments accountable for human rights violations resulting from environmental devastation. We also work closely with the United Nations to establish universal recognition of the right to a healthy environment and to defend victims of environmental destruction.

Earthjustice's International program played a key role in convincing a United Nations expert to find that, under international law, "all persons have the right to a healthy and ecologically sound environment." We have built on this important statement by providing detailed briefs in support of local communities seeking to hold US corporations responsible for destructive oil and mining activities. . . . In November 2002, the United Nations Committee on Economic, Social, and Cultural Rights recognized that the "human right to drinking water is fundamental for life and health."

In June 2002, the Organization of American States General Assembly passed a Resolution on Human Rights and Environment in the Americas, underscoring "the importance of studying the link . . . between the environment and human rights," and resolved, among other things, to "encourage institutional cooperation in the area of human rights and the environment in the framework of the Organization."

In October 2002, the Inter-American Commission on Human Rights held a "General Hearing" on the effects of environmental degradation on the realization of human rights in the hemisphere, for the first time formally and specifically addressing the linkages between human rights and the environment.

Of the 191 nations in the world, there are now 109 national constitutions that mention the protection of the environment or natural resources. One hundred of them recognize the right to a clean and healthy environment and/or the state's obligation to prevent environmental harm. Fifty-three constitutions explicitly recognize the right to a clean and healthy

> *environment, and 92 make it the duty of the national govern-*
> *ment to prevent harm to the environment. . . .*[37]

It appears that Earthjustice is making some headway on the international front, but I'm skeptical about US involvement. For example, how much was the advice of the UN heeded in the days leading up to the war in Iraq?

I again pursued the constitutional amendment angle.

The attorney informed me that a constitutional amendment is a very tough row to hoe. It requires two-thirds approval of both houses of congress and the three quarters approval of all the states. A near impossible task, he felt. I thanked him for his time and hung up feeling entirely deflated.

Upon reflection, I examined just how impossible this impossibility was. After the first ten amendments, which constituted the Bill of Rights, which were practically shooed in during the infancy of our government, there were seventeen more amendments. How impossible did any given one seem at the time it was proposed? What price was paid to make any given one a reality? Take for example the fifteenth amendment, which repealed slavery. Brother sometimes fought brother in the ugly Civil War to stop its passage. Lincoln was paradoxically respected and assassinated because of it. Both the 1962 Schlesinger News Agency poll of seventy-five historians and the 1982 *Chicago Tribune* poll of forty-nine historians rate him as our most revered (number one) president. Lincoln's memory lives on and he freed an entire race of people from a terrible injustice in one fell swoop. Where have you gone, Honest Abe? We sure as hell could use a fella like you around these parts these days.

If environmentalism doesn't become ranked as the defining issue of the twentieth century, as some journalists and historians feel it surely will, perhaps it will in this century. Is there another Lincoln out there with enough resolve and integrity to take the heat? Who among today's politicians would be willing to admit that an injustice has been done to the environment and would have the intestinal fortitude to try to right that wrong? Robert F. Kennedy, Jr. comes to mind. Surely, there must be others. Respectfully, I disagree with the attorney at Earthjustice who was kind enough to call me back. *A constitutional amendment is the way to go.* In fact, it may be the only thing that will have a meaningful and lasting effect on environmentalism in the twenty-first century.

Humans can be argumentative creatures. For every point or position that exists on any subject or in any field of endeavor there is an 180-degree opposing point or position. And so it is with environmentalism. Harvey Blatt's *Americas Environmental Report Card: Are We Making the Grade?*, published in 2005, can be counterbalanced against James Trefil's *Human Nature: A Blueprint for Managing the Earth—By People, For People.* Blatt's report card grades out like this:

Uses Water Responsibly	B-
Practices Flood Control	C
Safely Disposes of Garbage	B
Protects the Soil	C
Practices Energy Conservation	D
Tries to Stop Global Warming	D
Works to End Air Pollution	B
Takes Steps to Save Ozone Layer	A-
Safely Stores Nuclear Waste	C-
Overall Evaluation	C[38]

Blatt is to be commended on the depth of his research effort, which by all accounts, appears to have been exhaustive. While the book is couched in hopeful tones, the message is clear that there is a lot of room for improvement and that there is a tremendous amount of work to be done. This can only leave one to wonder, how do we go about getting the work done?

Trefil's book is much more hopeful than Blatt's. Trefil, if one were to judge by his impressive credentials, is quite possibly the smartest man in the world. I know I don't approach half of his intellectual breadth and I know that most other people don't either. While he presents some compelling arguments that hard line, deep green environmentalists need to take a serious look at, I couldn't help but notice that the book had an undercurrent of the tone of Dixy Lee Ray's (1990) *Trashing the Planet.* Ray played off a common theme that the scientific community postulated at the start of the seventies, that being that science and technology got us into this environmental mess and that science and technology would get us out of it. Trefil echoes this tone but pushes it one step further by stating that humans have a right to manage the planet and in so doing are simply following a logical sequence of events. The old book of Genesis sing-song of, "Multiply and fill the earth and subdue it. . . ." Writes Trefil at the conclusion of his book:

> So ready or not, like it or not, new advances in science will make us the gardeners of the planet. Nature, in the sense of wild places outside the realm of human care, will cease to exist. Our ancestors took the first step along this road thousands of years ago, when they began to remove themselves from nature. It is now our turn to take the step, to return to a nature that will be more human, more managed, than it has ever been. It

is our responsibility to decide what kind of world we want to live in, because we now have the power—and the responsibility—to bring that world into existence.

To those who believe that humans just don't have the ability to carry out this task, I would point out one thing. To turn away from the opportunity in front of us involves, in effect, making a bet against human ingenuity and intelligence.

Historically speaking, my friends, that is just about the worst bet anyone can make.[39]

I'm not betting against human ingenuity, for that is a proven commodity. I am, however, betting much more heavily that stupidity and greed will undermine human efforts at responsible earth management at every turn, which is even more of a proven human commodity. The why worry, we-are-smart-enough-to-figure-this-out proponents seem to rely on a replenishment of superior technological minds continuing to be born and moving up the ranks, which worries me because they apparently haven't noticed the stunning increase in newborn autism, which is primarily blamed on toxins in the environment. The possibility exists that because of various forms of poisoning, in particular mercury, that mankind to come may not be smarter and may, in fact, turn out to be dumber.

Green bashing is becoming quite popular among the scientific community. Trefil cites contemporary's Bjorn Lomborg's *The Skeptical Environmentalist* Litany which he paraphrases like this:

The environment is in poor shape. . . . Our resources are running out. The population is ever growing leaving less and less to eat. The air and water are becoming more polluted. The planet's species are becoming extinct in vast numbers. . . . We are defiling the Earth, the fertile topsoil is disappearing, we are paving over nature, destroying the wilderness, decimating the biosphere, and will end up killing ourselves in the process.[39]

I've paged through Lomborg's book at least a dozen times in various bookstores but it was so full of charts and statistics that it scared me off. To be fair, I haven't heard (by reading) him out, but I sense that the super-intelligent feel that the less intelligent should hang on and trust their every word because they're just plain smarter. I can't accept this because I've learned to trust in my gut and my gut tells me that, Litany or no Litany, the earth is in real trouble. A sense of environmentalism, if it's anything at all, is subliminal and driven by what our senses take in. I know the smog in Phoenix has gotten worse from when I first moved there (in 1976) to when I visit it today because I can see it with my own eyes. The same can be said for the way that land got chewed up when, at the end of the nineties, it was estimated that a mile of concrete was being laid daily to accommodate subdivision upon mindless subdivision.

The tiny town of Anza, population eight thousand, where I now live in the mountains of southern California is literally and figuratively at the crossroads of impending development. While rich developers are eyeing it as a "resort town," typical "strip" developers want to build out the main highway corridor before public opposition and the inevitable county restrictions that it will initiate closes their window of opportunity. I've started up a development company called ProAnza with a byline of "An Environmentally Sensitive Development Company." While I believe with all my heart that I can build meaningful communities that speak to nature and natural processes, my neighbors call me up and tell me that my byline is an "oxymoron." In all likelihood I'll be stuck sitting on the sidelines as big mega-developers come in here and blast out high density project after high density project with slick entry gates and solid masonry perimeter walls closing off entire sections of land to any form of wildlife migration and not giving a damn if lost habitat is replaced or restored or not. I'm not a Rhodes Scholar, but I'm not a blind man either. How much more proof do I need that the environment is going down the tubes faster than the intellectual scientific elite can tell me not to worry—they have got the whole thing covered?

More than the eco-elite, I worry about conservative America's overreaction to environmentalism.

I've just finished reading *The War Against the Greens* by David Helvarg and it was chilling, sobering, and challenging. Initially written in 1994, I'm amazed and somewhat ashamed that I hadn't come across it sooner. The book is a doggedly researched account of corporate America's assault on anyone who might stand in the way of their profits. The book highlights a battle waged in pranks, death threat phone calls, the car bombing of Judi Bari, and the extensive use of the widely preferred medium of anti-environmentalists—burning down the houses of their perceived adversaries. This has caused me to upgrade the insurance on my home and ask myself how far am I willing to go for what I believe in?

Financially, the odds against environmentalists seem insurmountable, as well over half of the world's one hundred largest economies are corporate and not national. The corporations can and often do spend ten dollars to every one expended by environmental organizations to fight their polluting and overharvesting interests. They can't be defeated with money and have significantly undermined being defeated by morality by adhering to the adage that, "The best defense is a good offense." To that end, they have now taken to firing the first shot and keeping them coming at the mere hint of any resistance to their near omnipotent power. To this end anti-enviro attorneys have taken to filing multimillion dollar lawsuits against environmentalists of modest economic means (most of us) in what have become known as SLAPPS, or Strategic Lawsuits Against Public Participation, in an effort to shut them up.

The anti-environmentalists have attached themselves like barnacles to the tenets of the "wise use" movement born of the wise use agenda promulgated as a twenty-five goal doctrine by Alan Gottlieb, a man of questionable ethics and intentions, in 1992. Wise use is wise by whose wisdom? This wisdom is rooted in the historical trends that have brought the earth to the brink of collapse through the desire to make money despite the costs. It has been and can still be said, not without considerable observation and provable examples, that money is the root of all evil. And evil in the form of disguised true agendas, misleading statistics, and out-and-out lies is now being cloaked in the main staple of the New Right—religious conviction. Apparently, pairing the stars and stripes with the crucifix equates to what's good for Americans. In the Book of Matthew (24:24), no less of an authority on human behavior than Jesus Christ stated that, many would come in his name preaching good but, in actuality, doing evil. The anti-environ- mentalists who have now aligned themselves with the New Right say that continued extraction of the earth's resources is an absolute necessity if we are to maintain our current lifestyle. They say that they exist in the "real world," which is to say that they exist in the now. They view the need to make money as an end unto itself and in so doing have risen the sta- tus of the corporation to that of Orwell's "Big Brother" in his classic novel *1984*.

James Watt, the anti-enviro poster child as Secretary of the

Interior in Ronald Regan's mid-eighties White House, summed up the anti-enviro viewpoint best when he said, *I do not know how many future generations we can count on before the Lord returns.* Utilizing religion to forward a live-for-today ideology is a preferred tactic of the New Right to discredit heathen greens at every turn. Anti-enviros feel that not only are greens misguided simpletons who obviously don't know how to succeed in the real world of business, worse yet, they fail to recognize that business is the Lord's work and exactly what was meant (again) in the Book of Genesis when He said, "Multiply and fill the earth and subdue it; you are masters blah blah blah blah." Masters of what? Anything that any given man can say is beneath him? Such a belief birthed slavery—man's ultimate brutality toward his fellow man. Being a master comes with some inherent responsibility. Masters must, for example, feed their pets or beasts of burden or they won't long be around to please and service them. So how do we feed the earth? How do we keep it alive? The answer is quite simply that we don't, and because of this, the question becomes: how long does the earth have to live?

Is the return of the Lord, so eloquently depicted in the Book of Revelation, a guaranteed occurrence? It's this belief that keeps the New Right in business. God will return before the well runs dry, before the fire goes out, before the earth gasps its last breath, so why worry? Two reasons. First, the Bible, while intended to proclaim the word of God, was written by mere men who are fallible and can be misguided. It's conceivable that He could have been misquoted. Secondly, it's just as conceivable that someone (many ones) among mankind had an axe to grind and saw the written word of the Bible as the perfect vehicle with which to do the grinding.

The older I get the more I've supposedly learned, but all

aging has really taught me is how much I don't know, how much there is out there that I will never know. Although I still believe that the Bible, or more specifically, Jesus' message of love in the New Testament, is the most important book in existence, I don't believe with unfaltering certainty that its aggregate messages are infallible. Mistakes could have been made.

Other books are vying for the number two position on the importance to mankind chart. Early on in the environmental movement, books like Rachel Carson's *Silent Spring*, Paul Ehrilich's *The Population Bomb*, and later, Mark Hertsquarrd's *Earth Odyssey* and Alice Outwater's *Water,* forced us to assess mankind's place on earth.

The list goes on and on and on. Just like the focus of the Bible, these works are about mankind's survival on planet earth. The newer works also express concern for the survival of the "lower species." The primary point of divergence is that, unlike the Bible, they are not certain whether the species *homo sapiens* will meet its end by God's hand or its own.

Silent Spring is still on the shelves at the local bookstore. Since its publication in 1962 it has sold over two million copies and spawned widespread controversy and debate. Some say it was and still is a manifesto that changed the world. Others say it gave flight to the emotionally charged sixties. The work challenged convention, challenged the establishment's position that what it did was always for our own good. Its underlying message is that research and those that read the research should look at the facts and make their own conclusions. This, coupled with the immensely unpopular war in south Viet Nam, birthed a generation of dissidents, birthed the Green Revolution, birthed the possible rebirth of a dying earth. The jury is still out as to whether or not this rebirth happened soon enough.

The widespread civil unrest of the sixties caught the eye of the nation and was fought with Nixon's silent majority and Reagan's trickle down theory. In short, the conservative Republicans, for the most part, laughed off the early days of the Green Revolution as a phenomenon that merely transformed beatniks into hippies. They breathed a huge sigh of relief when hippies became yuppies. The desire for the finer things in life, as it usually did, would defeat youthful indignation.

The only problem was that enough members of the faltering Green Revolution remained indignant enough to become a royal pain in the ass. Whistle blowers and tree huggers made the establishment uncomfortable. How could they maintain the status quo with all these noisy, distracting environmentalists sticking their oar in at every turn? Then they hit upon the answer. They would fight fire with fire.

The early successes of the Green Revolution were not lost on its opponents. They studied the organization and movements of early grassroots efforts and were unpleasantly surprised when something started to come out of nothing. There was a purity of spirit and an honesty of intent in the environmental movement that they envied and, with imitation being the sincerest form of flattery, they decided to emulate— "Many will come in my name."

Backlash to the environmental movement is difficult to ascertain when it's housed in groups whose acronyms and names sound like the names of pro-environmental groups. AER—Alliance of Environment and Resources, AFC— American Freedom Coalition, AFRA—American Forest Resource Alliance, CARE—Concerned Alaskans for

Resources and Environment, CREA—Coalition of Republican Environment Advocates, EAGLE—Alabamians Guardians of our Land and Environment, ECO— Environmental Conservation Organization, FLOC—Fairness to Land Owners Committee, FREE—Foundation for Research of Economics and the Environment, LICA—Land Improvement Contractors Association, PFW—People for the West!, SEPP—Science and Environmental Policy Project, WE CARE WIRE—Wilderness Impact Research Foundation. All of these groups sound like they may have been formed to do something good for the environment. Let me assure you that they were not. Although they sound like EPA, (Environmental Protection Agency) and WWF (World Wildlife Fund) their intent is for economic, and not environmental, benefit.

Perhaps the biggest rip-off of an environmental group's name came from the Sahara Club, which is an obvious sarcastic twist on the Sierra Club's name. The Sahara Club was formed explicitly to oppose the Desert Bill that was primarily backed by the Sierra Club and which ultimately set aside the Mohave National Preserve and put an end to the Barstow, California to Las Vegas, Nevada Thanksgiving weekend motorcycle race. Rick Sieman, Sahara Club founder, published a newsletter that lived in infamy as radical opposition to the Desert Bill and called for a massive protest ride in 1990. An interesting side note is that funding for the newsletter was at least one-third provided by environmentalists who bought it in an attempt to keep a watchful eye on the opposition. "Many will come in my name. . . ."

All of this causes me to consider founding CRAPEO (Center for the Removal of Annoying Pretend Environmental Organizations). I must, of course, weigh this desire against the inevitable backlash or as the highly quotable James Watt put it, *If the trouble from environmentalists cannot be solved in the jury box, or the ballot box, perhaps the cartridge box should be used.*[36] This utterance, or flatulence—take your pick—spewed forth when Watt was in office, is certainly revealing of the depth and breadth of the hatred that some of the opposition has toward the environmental movement.

It's not surprising to me at all that the anti-enviros apparently have the upper hand on the enviros because of the love of money, which borders on phobia in the United States. The sad fact is that altruism will never defeat it.

Returning to the premise put forth at the start of this chapter, it seems to me that the only way enviros are ever going to win this war (besides accepting the fact that they are at war) is to define clean air and water as an inalienable right and have it recognized as such as an amendment to the Constitution of the United States of America. It seems utterly absurd that if President George W. Bush can pry into the personal lives of US citizens and attack gay marriages, then environmentalists who are championing the much more *public* issue of clean air and water shouldn't be able to do likewise by employing the same tactic.

If an environmental precedent can be set via a constitutional amendment accommodating these two issues, a day in court for all the other environmental issues will surely follow. And such a grand day will provide the spark that ignites and mobilizes the Green Revolution.

Epilogue: Quotes

Soon afterwards He left that section of the country and returned with his disciples to Nazareth, his home town. The next Sabbath he went to the synagogue to teach, and the people were astonished at his wisdom and his miracles because he was just a local man like themselves. "He's not better than we are," they said. "He's just a carpenter, Mary's boy, and a brother of James and Joseph, Judas and Simon. And his sisters live right here among us." And they were offended!

Then Jesus told them. "A prophet is honored everywhere except in his home town and among his relatives and by his own family." And because of their unbelief he couldn't do any mighty miracles among them except to place his hands on a few sick people and heal them. And he could hardly accept the fact that they wouldn't believe in him.

Then he went out among the villages teaching. And he called his twelve disciples together and sent them out two by two with power to cast out demons. He told them to take nothing with them except their walking sticks—no food, no knapsack, no money, not even an extra pair of shoes or a change of clothes. "Stay at one home in each village—don't shift around from house to house while you are there," he said. "And whenever a village won't accept you or listen to you, shake off the dust from your feet as you leave; it is a sign that you have abandoned it to its fate."[40]

Book of Mark
The Living Bible

According to a national bipartisan poll conducted in early 2004, 65 percent of American voters would be willing to support modest increases in taxes to pay for programs to protect water quality, wildlife habitat, and neighborhood parks. There was particularly strong support for conservation funding measures from Latino voters—77 percent. An earlier survey by the National Association of Realtors found that more than 80 percent of voters support preserving farmland, natural areas, stream corridors, true wilderness areas, and historic sites in areas under pressure from development, although support decreased among lower-

income residents when property tax increases were added in other survey questions.[41]

Nature Friendly Communities
Christopher Duerksen
Cara Snyder

So, too, it might have been only a matter of time before the real-estate dreams of the American mainstream spilled into the Salton Sink, drawn there by the accidental sea and the images of shorefront luxury and frolic that its waters made possible. The dreams that ended in that unlikely place descended from others that had flowed west in a human current all the way from Europe. That current of dream had promised landownership for countless thousands who might never have imagined owning land except on the broad American continent. No one checked the progress of that river of dreams for long, not for the sake of the land's previous Indian owners, though the attempt was repeatedly made, nor for the sake of wise settlement and the rational use of land, though that attempt was also repeatedly made. The current of people's hope and hunger for land flowed over or around every obstacle it encountered on the long trip west across the continent. And then in California, it hit the limit of the land.[42]

Salt Dreams
William de Buys
Joan Myers

The real estate developer, despite the mounting opposition, has an instinct to build programmed deep inside him. . . . Like a mountain lion protecting her cubs, he has an almost maternal instinct towards the construction process. It's who he is, and if you think that you're going to stop him you had better be ready to put up your dukes.[20]

Environmental Cognizance
John C. Krieg

Epilogue

I wrote about the real estate perils facing the Anza Valley in the epilogue of *Econation* and skipped town leaving the readership wondering if what was about to happen would indeed happen sooner or later. Well, for the foreseeable future, say the next four years, not much of anything will happen, and then, after that, the inevitable will happen—Anza will get "whored out."

Numbed by helplessness and ineptitude, I sat on the sidelines as anyone with an opinion weighed in on the "development issue" of the Anza Valley. Articles, pro and con, crisscrossed like bullets in a Wild West range war in the two local newspapers, making for entertaining reading and lending a carnival-like atmosphere, which opened the way for third district Riverside County Supervisor Jeff Stone to bring his traveling circus to town.

The members of our fair community packed the isles at the community center as Stone played to the predominately over-seventy audience, waxing poetic on issues such as prison reform even though we have no criminals to speak of. Criminals being the type of thing that gets the elderly mighty upset, it's good that Supervisor Stone has a plan to take care of them if and when they do appear. This discussion and the time expended to introduce his excessive staff chewed up the first part of the meeting, leaving the second part wide open for heated questions about our inadequate road system and a few odd comments, here and there, about problems and shenanigans at the local dump.

Supervisor Stone blamed the problems with the roads and just about everything else on greedy real estate developers with "deep pockets." He kept hammering home that development would not occur unless developers paid infrastructure costs up-front, which was, after all, their inherent responsibility. Knowing that I would only be given the opportunity to speak once, I resisted the urge to ask why the county wasn't obligated to pay any infrastructure costs in that we were being heavily taxed, fined, and ridiculed by this government entity at every turn. Other counties in other parts of America pay infrastructure costs outright or at least split them with real estate developers so, to my way of thinking, why were things so different in Riverside County? But then I gazed upon that excessive staff all sitting upright and expertly in front of us and I pretty much had my answer. Supervisor Stone's road guy (Boy, he had a lot of guys and a few gals.) did say that he would look into things and that pretty much quieted everyone down, leading me to whisper to my wife, "Everyone's going to travel on a good road to No-where's-ville."

When I finally did get to speak I asked Supervisor Stone about the fate of downtown Anza or what I like to refer to as the "village core." I cited the county's own somewhat sketchy master plan and its "rural village overlay" as an avenue to creating a community dialogue as to how development should occur in this area and what the general facade of the downtown area should be. Mr. Stone smugly said the rural village overlay was misleading, although he didn't say why. He said that such "things" caused problems for the county although he didn't say why, leading me to assume that the problem was that someone at the county would have to do some real work in reviewing submittals. He did say something about how the downtown area should have been "specifically zoned" but didn't really say why, leading me to think probably because if it had been "specifically zoned" it wouldn't have caused anyone at the county to do any real work. Stone's "legal guy" (Boy, he had a lot of guys and a few gals.) did answer a few of my questions much to his relief and the relief of the audience because there was nothing left for me to do but shut up and sit down. I whispered to my wife, "This is biblical because a prophet is never recognized in his homeland," and "Everything he says about developers is doubly true of politicians."

Vicki Conover, once again, summed up the proceedings in her fair-minded article in the *High Country Journal (HCJ)*.

5/1/05
DEVELOPER'S STONEWALLED
NOTHIN'S GONNA HAPPEN OUT HERE
SAYS SUPERVISOR STONE
by Vicki Conover
  In a crowd-pleasing performance at the April 13th "Town Hall" meeting hosted by the Anza Valley Municipal Advisory Council, Riverside County Supervisor Jeff Stone declared that the people have spoken, he has listened, and what he has heard is they want to keep their rural community intact and "just want to be left alone."
  Throughout the evening, Mr. Stone repeatedly expressed his disdain for developers and for former supervisor Jim Venable. "Most developers I've worked with are not very honest," he said. And he vowed that he will not push development through as did Jim Venable. Mr. Stone also criticized Mr. Venable for

not requiring developers to fund infrastructure to support the development (i.e. roads, utilities) and have that infrastructure in place before construction begins.

Mr. Stone reinforced his "no development" message through the curt tone of his replies to two audience members who spoke in favor of a specific plan being created for the development of the "Rural Village Overlay" (central Anza).

John Krieg, who is interested in creating the architectural plan for the Anza village, asked if the results of the required studies (i.e. water, environmental impact) paid for by one entity could be used by other entities.

After complaining that these overlays have created problems for the county because they're too wide open and instead should have been specifically zoned, Mr. Stone's [actually his legal guy's] *reply was yes but there is a time limit on a study's validity, usually one or two years. He then added that an entity who hires a private company to conduct these studies can pay that company to get the results they want, and the county knows which companies are not reputable.*

Chris Engholm, Chairman of the Anza Valley Building Association (AVBA), which would like to create and implement a specific plan for the Anza village, introduced himself and AVBA's ideas.

Mr. Stone informed Mr. Engholm that County Planning Director Bob Johnson would listen to AVBA's proposal but when it is presented to him, he will reject it, and the other four supervisors on the board will follow him in voting against it. "Nothing's gonna happen out here," vowed Mr. Stone to the audience.

Well maybe "nothing" is too strong a word.

When asked by an audience member, "How left alone can Anza expect to be and for how long?" the supervisor replied, "As long as I'm in office I will not approve a development project unless infrastructure is completed first." He said road building and road improvement should be funded by develop-

ers and also stated that he "wants development that's an asset not a liability."

Chris Engholm when asked by HCJ for a response to Supervisor Stone's statements offered the opinion that Mr. Stone will not allow growth. "In fact, there is already a great deal of growth underway," said Mr. Engholm, "except it's proceeding in the typical disorganized manner like it has in Hemet and Banning. What a specific plan for the rural village overlay will do is preserve the qualities we all like about Anza Valley and prevent the piecemeal development. . . ." [43]

It should be noted that Mr. Krieg was also asked for a reply by an out of town newspaper, to which he stated such things as, "Smug _ _ _ _ _ _ _" and "We are living in the Stone Age." These comments were apparently found un-newsworthy. To be fair, I really think that there are good developers and bad developers just as there are good politicians and bad politicians. As with everything in life most people fall within the shades of gray that exist somewhere between good and bad. So, for now, the Anza Valley is living in the Stone Age, but what bothers me the most is what this smug man and his beliefs truly represent. In actuality, he is the living embodiment of big conservative Republican government that can only be defeated or swayed by big money. The small local developers who live here and care about this place aren't rich enough to get in the game. I'm certainly locked out of any chance to make a difference. Those citizens gullible enough to think that this man really has their best interests at heart are in for a rude awakening when the first big mega-developer rolls in here and rolls over them. Sure, such a developer may abide by the Stone Age rules of paying up-front for infrastructure expenses, but he will extract his revenge thru extremely high-density development to recoup his costs.

Citizens of the Anza Valley, just wait until you get a load of what living in the Stone Age really means and rest assured that the carnival will come back to town but the tickets will be more expensive and the show won't be as good.

As Stone and his traveling circus of political experts temporarily left town I was left to ponder my future as a developer in Anza, which is to more appropriately say, I have no future. I had spewed forth with my opinions and "vision" in the *High Country Journal* and had even kept a running verbal skirmish going with the president of the Municipal Advisory Council (MAC) about who got to speak and who didn't (namely me) at a previous heated town meeting. Anyone in town who cared to read about my opinions could have easily found out exactly where I stood—no one cared. I wasn't invited to speak or present any plans nor was I consulted by the county, the MAC, or any given man in the street even though, to my knowledge, I was the only full-time resident of the Anza Valley with any planning knowledge whatsoever. Issues concerning the downtown area still concerned me, so imagine my relief when this article appeared in *HCJ*.

6/1/05
TIME TO DECIDE
Anza Village Center—Yes or No?
by: Vicki Conover
  Frank Miller and his wife, Jane Grabowski-Miller, are not real estate developers plotting to exploit Anza for their own profit; they are architects and planners offering their knowledge, experience, and leadership to help Anza residents build a village center—if Anza residents want a village center.
  "It's entirely in your hands," said Mr. Miller to the audience at the May 11th Anza Valley Municipal Advisory

Council meeting (AVMAC), at which the Millers were guest speakers.

But they didn't just speak; they listened, they answered questions honestly, and they asked the question: Do you want a village center?

By a show of hands, the answer was an overwhelming "yes." That "yes," however, only represented the wishes of the approximately 40 residents who attended the meeting. What do the rest of you want? If you care to have a say in guiding the growth of Anza, come to the June 8th AVMAC meeting at which the Millers will appear again, this time bringing with them Riverside County Director of Planning, Robert Johnson.

At this meeting, Mr. Miller will again present his village center design as an example of what Anza could have, the Millers and Mr. Johnson will answer all questions, and by the end of the evening it is expected that the audience will have reached a consensus regarding that question. Do you want a village center? The MAC will convey the answer to Supervisor Jeff Stone.

If that answer is "yes," the next steps would be for residents to determine the exact location for the village center within the RCIP—designated "rural village overlay" (approximately 2000 acres in central Anza) and for Mr. Miller to initiate discussions with overlay land owners and then with Mr. Stone.

But as Frank Miller made clear, if residents want a village center, he alone can't make it happen. "It takes a lot of determination by the residents," he said. "You have to muster that determination."

Those 40 residents at the May MAC meeting seemed ready to muster after seeing Mr. Miller's village center design. They were especially impressed with his proposal to start small and grow as the population grows, yet keep the planning (but not the construction) ahead of the growth. Mr. Miller pointed out that, because the process will be so gradual, spanning many years, the planning needs to be flexible.

The audience also liked Frank Miller's idea of the village center being located, not along Highway 371, but perpendicular or parallel to it. This would essentially be a "Main Street" involving about three or four blocks. The portion of the highway within the overlay could become a slow traffic area with stoplights and a 25 mph speed limit, which would encourage passers-through to notice the highway businesses and the adjacent village center.

Frank Miller's overall concept for the village center is a traditional small town walking "Main Street" comprised of "mixed use" two or three story buildings with shops and services at street level, and offices and residences upstairs (people living within the village creates a more friendly and safe environment). And, yes, there could be a grocery store. The Millers have, in fact, spent the last ten years creating a village center just like this for the residents of Middleton, Wisconsin.

Although the Millers are not members of the Anza Valley Building Association (AVBA), they say their proposal is not in conflict with AVBA's, it's just on a smaller scale. Pat DeMartino, AVBA board member, agrees. "We have the same goal," she stated, "but AVBA would like an overall architectural plan for the entire overlay."

The goal AVBA and the Millers have in common is to see Anza's unique character and sense of community embraced and enriched by a village center. It's now time for Anza residents to decide if they too share this goal, or if they'd rather see a mish-mash of strip development up and down the highway.

Come to the AVMAC meeting Wednesday, June 8th, 7:00 p.m. at the Community Hall.[43]

I had met Frank Miller, who is a resident of Wisconsin, at the inaugural meeting of the Anza Valley Builders Association (AVBA) three months earlier. I was impressed with his credentials, which included past involvement with the University of Wisconsin's Department of Landscape Architecture and

Land Planning. This is one of the top three schools in the country in my estimation. I had sent him my "package" of drawings and newspaper articles, to which there was no immediate response.

I had been at the earlier May 11th meeting where Frank Miller and his wife presented their "vision" for a downtown center. I spoke up then stating that although it was a nice enough looking plan I felt it was in the wrong location.

Vicki Conover failed to make note of my dissenting remarks in her article. She also was not one-hundred percent correct in stating that the Miller's aren't real estate developers, as they own approximately forty acres of land here in Anza and plan full well to have it serve it's "highest and best purpose."

Upon receiving my e-mail from the MAC inviting me to attend the upcoming June 8th meeting, I e-mailed this letter to the president of the MAC.

May 18, 2005
RE: R.C.I.P. Overlay—Village Center.
Jackie:

I don't want to see a Village Center that runs perpendicular to Highway 371. I do want to see a Village Center that encompasses the existing shops and stores that are already here parallel to 371. In my newspaper article of January 1st in the High Country Journal I outlined my vision.

First of all, I feel that a true nonprofit redevelopment agency needs to be formed to help existing business owners defray the costs of creating a unified building facade/street scene and to upgrade parking. Second, I would advocate parking in the rear of facilities to physically and visually take the vehicles away from the street. Third, I would urge that traffic be slowed to twenty-five miles per hour or even fifteen miles per hour through the village center and a bypass road (roads) cre-

ated around it. In addition, a pedestrian overpass across 371 is not a bad idea and provides a level of safety.

The fundamental flaw of the overlay is that it is too linear and, by virtue of its shape, will encourage linear, along the highway development, which every planner that has come in here says we should avoid. How do we avoid it if this is the only thing the boundaries will allow?

I feel the Village Center should extend primarily from Hill Street in the east to Bahrman Road in the west, approximately one thousand feet north of the existing Hardware/Variety stores and extend south to the north boundary of the Cahuilla Indian Reservation. I would suggest that the north/south axis be Contreras Road, which already contains the park/school house, new Mormon Church (reasonably well done), and the Anza Village Market, which is not that bad and could easily be improved.

Most of the big city planners want to reinvent the wheel and see money as no object. They also point to Julian as a model but fail to realize (or admit) that Julian was a fortunate accident that occurred not because of any great planning effort but because its physical constraints forced it to be concentric in nature and discouraged sprawl.

Anza would be well advised to think concentrically and not linearly if it wants to establish a village character. Historically, towns stayed compact so that goods and services were within walking distance. If this simple concept were adopted as the thrust for Anza's Village Center, sprawl would be kept in check. If Anza is to draw tourism, then large areas for overflow surface parking will have to be provided. This could be metered and the funds generated put toward civic projects.

It's easy for planners to pick out a piece of virgin land and say, "Let's design on this blank canvas and create perfection." This really isn't any great challenge but it totally ignores what is. If the citizens of this town truly care about this town then they can't turn their backs on the existing shop and storeowners who have historically supported it. This one fact dictates *that the proposed Village Center be located where it has always been situated, but has not really been finished.*

Two excellent books that discuss these topics at length are The Geography of Nowhere *by William Howard Kuntsler and* The Next American Metropolis *by Peter Calthorpe.*

In closing, I appreciate your efforts on behalf of the towns- people and certainly hope you will continue on with the MAC.

Sincerely yours,
John C. Krieg

The day prior to the June 8th meeting I received this e- mail from (I can only assume) the president of the MAC.

Reminder:
June 8, 7:00 p.m. Community Hall
AVMAC Meeting

Speakers:
Robert Johnson, Director of Planning, Riverside County.
Frank Miller, Architect, Planner, Home Owner.

"Does Anza Want a Village?" Please remember that this question will be based on the premise that the village will be placed perpendicular to Highway 371 and that all County requirements (water, infrastructure, impact, etc.) have been met. Mr. Johnson and Mr. Miller will take your questions after about three minutes of announcements from the MAC. The evening belongs to the residents of Anza who care how we grow.

So this is how it was, huh? I took the message to mean that if you didn't support Frank Miller's plan then don't show up. I certainly didn't support his plan. I had mulled it over since his May 11th presentation and decided that it surely would have been better than *no plan* and that if this was what the community wanted then I would lend help if asked to do so wherever I could. But the MAC e-mail insulted me. How does a supposed agency representing a government entity (Riverside County) get to stack the deck like this? I also wondered just how many other residents of the Anza Valley received an e-mail such as this? Enough rejection was enough rejection and I didn't attend. I and anyone else who didn't attend were apprised of the proceedings in the June 15th edition of the *HCJ*.

6/15/05
RESIDENTS TAKE ONE "TINY STEP"
AND ONE BIG "LEAP OF FAITH"
TOWARD VILLAGE CENTER
by Vicki Conover

Valid concerns were raised and some anger was expressed, but in the end, a consensus was reached favoring the start of the long complex process of creating an Anza Village Center.

Approximately 100 residents attended the June 8th Anza Valley Municipal Advisory Council (AVMAC) meeting to participate in deciding whether or not to support the Village Center concept envisioned by architect and planner Frank Miller.

That concept involves about 200 acres within the "overlay" (downtown Anza) situated, not on the highway, but perpendicular to it. It would be a walking village with ample centralized parking, and featuring a "Main Street" three or four blocks long, lined with diagonal parking and two or three-story "mixed use" buildings (offices, shops, residences). Surrounding Main Street would be high density residences, perhaps including an apartment building or assisted living facility.

As to the exact location of the Village, Mr. Miller corrected the statement he made at the May MAC meeting in which he said residents would decide the location. "All land owners within the overlay must have equal access to having the Village Center on their land," he said this time, and he added that the county will also have a say in the location.

Mr. Miller suggested that several smaller "Neighborhood Centers" could be built throughout the remainder of the overlay to support the Village Center. He also suggested that Anza's Village could be a model for other growing Riverside County communities, which should be an incentive for the county to support the Anza project.

Riverside County Director of Planning, Robert Johnson, attended the meeting at the request of Frank Miller to answer questions from the county perspective. Mr. Johnson stated up front that he is impressed with Mr. Miller's Village concept for Anza and implied disdain for the alternative, which he said would be "strip development like Florida Avenue in Hemet." He said the county has no ideas of its own as to what should happen within Anza's overlay and the community will be listened to if they make a strong statement to the county.

Mr. Johnson did not respond directly to the audience's demand for a comprehensive water study, but he is well aware of Anza's water and roads issues, which present obstacles to growth. He related that when developer Robert Dyson came to him with plans for Anza and Garner Valley he told Mr. Dyson two things: "Don't talk to us until you know you have water" and "We need to know the transportation system can support a larger population."

In addition to those water and road issues, meeting attendees also were concerned that their property taxes would have to be raised to pay for the roadwork, water and sewage systems, and additional sheriff and fire protection.

Mr. Johnson conceded that, yes, there will probably be more taxes but he pointed out that the inevitable strip development along the highway would also increase taxes. He mentioned that a CSA (County Service Area) could be developed and residents within the CSA would be taxed. He also stated, more than once, that Supervisor Stone is adamant that developers must pay for infrastructure. Frank Miller added that even if residents don't take the initiative to guide the growth, the growth is going to happen anyway and taxes will be raised anyway.

When questioned about the high density housing aspect of the Village Center proposal, Mr. Miller replied that high density housing is needed to support the Village Center, but that housing would only be within the overlay, which is zoned for it, and he is confident the rest of Anza will remain 5-acre minimum rural residential. That's the purpose of the overlay plan and the Village Center concept: to keep the density in one compact area, which allows for lots of open space surrounding it.

Expressing understanding of all the concerns of the audience, Frank Miller advised that if anyone needs everything figured out in advance they should vote no on the Village Center. "It takes trust, it takes a leap of faith, to say you want a Village Center," he said.

At that, MAC Chair Jackie Spanley asked for a show of hands, stressing that this informal vote is being taken on the assumption that all studies have been completed; she also assured the audience that their vote was not a commitment. "Would you like to maintain the status quo" and "let whatever happens happen?" asked Mrs. Spanley. Or would you like to "take the first tiny step forward" toward having a Village Center? Nearly everyone voted to take the step.

Jackie Spanley has just announced that Robert Johnson will return to facilitate the August 10th AVMAC meeting, which will focus on defining "the ten things we most want to see happen in Anza."[43]

I wish the residents of the tiny town of Anza all the luck in the world in directing their development future. In some small way I might yet get involved but I sincerely doubt it. From where I stand I don't think they recognize the real threat.

Mega-real estate developers look for setups like this. An unincorporated small town dependent on county services where the county seat is sixty miles away. A citizenry not much united on anything. A county supervisor who talks the talk to the local elderly population but won't walk the walk when the mega-developer comes a-calling with his mega-dollars. One of the last Western range towns is set up like beer bottles on a log waiting to be mowed down. Who will the shooter be? Someone with a big political rifle and loads of cash. Definitely not me. A prophet is never recognized in his homeland. I have a family to feed and a stalled career to nourish and I must move on. But where? Where will things be different than they are here in ho dunk Riverside County? Imperial County on the western shores of the Salton Sea where developers and planned growth are welcome—that's where.

Imperial County lies south of Riverside County and east of San Diego County. Since the 1900s its centrally located Imperial Valley has been known as, "the salad bowl of America." Here the politics of Western water and brown labor have a storied legacy well documented in William deBuy's *Salt Dreams: Land and Water in Low Down California*. The Salton Sea referred to by deBuys as, "A Sea of Unintention," was formed between the years 1905–1907 as record rainy weather and human folly merged to produce an oddity of nature as well as an oddity of life.

The mighty Colorado River, now referred to as, "the West's last watering hole," once flowed from the western escarpments of the Rocky Mountains through Colorado, New Mexico, Utah, Arizona, and California to the Sea of Cortez on the eastern flank of the Baja Peninsula. The Colorado River delta that occurred from present day Yuma, Arizona to the river's mouth represented a rich and diverse ecosystem such as

America has not seen since the river was dammed in the name of progress (agriculture/electricity) and flood control.

The sea that was formed at the start of the twentieth century was first destined to become a recreational haven and then became an environmental problem of ever worsening proportions. Salton City was an ambitious master planned middle-class community established in 1951 when founder M. Penn Phillips threw a massive kickoff party on May 21st, 1951 and delivered this speech to potential real estate investors.

> *Ladies and gentlemen, suppose someone handed you four million dollars and said, "There's plenty more where that came from, but take this as a starter and plan the world's perfect city."... What you see around you, is like the tip of an iceberg. We see only one-seventh above the surface, but the broad base of men, money, and imagination is there.... Think about the picture you have in mind of the perfect place, and the ideal setting. Wouldn't it be much like this? A place ringed by snow-capped mountains and bathed in warm sunshine winter and summer, and cooled by sea breezes. A place where you could go swimming in warm, smooth saltwater the year round. Or boating. Or water skiing. Or just loaf on the beach under the clearest of blue skies, breathing air so clean you can see for fifty miles. A place where you can ride horseback. Or hunt. Or just sip a tall, cool drink. There is such a place coming to life on the shores of our largest inland body of water: Salton Riviera on the Salton Sea. A place where you can buy now for enjoyment and hold for income and a share of the profits in what may become the most fabulous resort city in the world. I have never been able to stand on that rise of land above the Salton Sea without seeing a great resort city. Now our dream is coming to life.*[43]

Phillips' commission hungry sales force whipped the land investors to a frenzy by ushering them into presentation tents, and flying them over numbered lots. Within weeks five thousand lots had been gobbled up and there were still fifteen thousand more waiting in standing inventory. M. Penn Phillips made a killing on the shores of the Salton Sea and was poised to rake in even bigger profits when he surprised everyone in the real estate world by selling all his remaining interests to the Dallas-based Holly Corporation in 1960. Holly Corporation carried the torch into the seventies by which time all of the platted lots had been sold but, not to worry, there was more land that could be re-zoned where those lots came from.

All was not well in real estate paradise. Fluctuating water levels, inexplicable shifts in demographics, and a paper vision too grand to be executed in reality all contributed to Salton City never becoming what M. Penn Phillips had envisioned—until now. Now this dog is about to have its day. The fundamental difference between Imperial County and Riverside County is that the former welcomes planned growth while the latter is overwhelmed with it. I made a futile attempt to contact third district Riverside County Supervisor Jeff Stone shortly before he took office and was filtered through several layers of staff before someone eventually committed to have one of his "key staff" contact me, which actually did happen—eight weeks hence. In a curt, insensitive, two-minute conversation I was brusquely brushed aside by this "key staff" and made to feel I may never talk to the good supervisor unless I verbally accosted him at a town hall meeting and we all know how well that went.

On the other hand, I have fourth district Imperial County Supervisor Gary Wyatt's cell phone number and I can call him day or night and he's happy to hear from me. One views the developer as the great Satan while the other views the developer as the second coming. If you were trying to get a project off the ground where would you choose to work?

The Salton Sea, if it is anything, is a phenomenon of the desert and to understand the essence of the desert means to live in it. To see it when the photographers don't, at three o'clock in the afternoon when the light gives all it touches a patina of dullness and not a creature stirs—except me and others like me, a bastardization of the obvious laws of nature. Sunrise was beautiful and so too will be sunset but if one finds beauty in truth one will look at the desert at three P.M. in July and realize he really doesn't belong.

This is what I share with the Salton Sea; we are both accidents upon the landscape, and under normal circumstances, what we are supposed to be. Even a life formed of accident has to be lived and I have no life if I have no projects. Realizing this means also realizing that there are no better projects to work on than those that I create for myself. And so it is I come upon this project and this landscape of weirdoes, has-beens, never-weres, ex-hippies, ex-yuppies, dreamers, schemers, burnouts, and the eternally optimistic. The Salton Sea draws them all to her shores. With the eloquent words of William deBuys not withstanding and the forewarnings of many far more astute than I going unheeded, I penned this executive summary for our development investors to join us in revamping the closed Salton City Golf Course with 140 attendant housing lots and hoped for the best:

EXECUTIVE SUMMARY

The Salton Sea and its attendant communities are now entering their centennial celebration. The Sea was formed in

1905 when the Colorado River altered its normal course into the Sea of Cortez and jumped its banks and flowed generally northwestward into the Salton Sink. This is an event that had occurred, on and off, for centuries. During a two-year period of unprecedented high rainfall the Sea acquired its present day average dimensions of thirty miles in length and ten miles in width. To gain perspective, it is roughly one-third larger than Lake Tahoe. The Sea is only an average of sixty-five feet deep, and owing to the fact that it spread out over an ancient ocean depression, the water has become quite saline, and at current levels, is twenty-five percent saltier than Pacific Ocean water. This salinity has not caused the sea to become "dead" however. In fact, the Salton Sea is considered a major sports fishery with abundant croaker, sargo, tilapia, and the renowned fighting fish, the Orange-mouth covina.

After the Southern Pacific Railroad mounted a Herculean effort to build a dike that forced the Colorado River back into its historic channel in 1907, it was suspected that the newly formed water body would gradually recede and eventually dry out. Such was not the case, however, as it was learned that the Sea lies at the bottom of a 7,851 square mile watershed with no outlet. Today, ninety percent of the inflow into the Sea comes from agricultural runoffs and the remaining ten percent comes from ground water, scant rainfall, and urban waste-water. For over one hundred years the Sea has maintained a level plus or minus ten feet of its current 227 feet below sea level elevation. In short, the Salton Sea is here to stay.

A large water body created in the desert by an act of God was looked at as a boon by modern man. Hollywood came a calling in the 1920s and '30s, producing such movies as Beau Geste *starring Gary Cooper. In the late thirties and early forties, speedboat racing took off and the Sea was the site of five world records. Oceanic fishes were transplanted in the fifties and the Sea became a major sports fishery. In the early fifties M. Penn Phillips established a nineteen thousand-plus housing community on the west shore called Salton City. Boasting a*

181

modern layout even by today's standards, Salton City offered marinas, a country club, and an eighteen-hole championship golf course. Other north shore communities boasted of glamorous marinas and the Sea experienced a heyday during which an estimated five hundred thousand vacationers and thrill seekers visited it annually. The Salton City Golf Course hosted Bing Crosby, Jerry Lewis, the Marx Brothers, The Beach Boys, and a young, up-and-coming Sonny Bono. It looked for all the world like Salton City was poised to be launched into the economic stratosphere, but faster than you could say, "I got you babe," it went bust.

Three things contributed to Salton City's rapid decline. First and foremost were unpredictable fluctuations in water level. Apparently floating marinas were unheard of in the fifties. Second, was the rapid increase in competing fresh water recreational lakes throughout southern California, the apparent offspring of America's dam building craze. And third, rumors of rampant pollution caused visitors to stay away in droves. The bottom entirely fell out when the Salton City Golf Course was officially closed in 1980. The pollution rumors persisted to the close of the twentieth century and, like most rumors, caused more economic than physical damage. The Salton Sea and down and out Salton City looked like goners for sure except for the efforts of one Mary Bono.

Dedicating her efforts to deceased husband Sonny, Mary changed the name of the Sea's National Wildlife Refuge (established November 25th, 1930) to the Sonny Bono Salton Sea National Wildlife Refuge.

The south end of the Salton Sea is home to over four hundred species of migrating birds and an important rest stop for intercontinental avian travelers. While California leads the nation in loss of wetland habitat, losing ninety-one percent of its overall acreage from five million acres in 1800 to just 450,000 acres today, the forgotten about Salton Sea, which lies directly in the path of the Pacific Coast Flyway, has risen in biological importance to the station of the number one bird habitat in the U.S.

Primarily due to the thrust of Congresswoman Bono's Salton Sea environmental and "clean up" efforts, the Redlands Institute at the University of Redlands in conjunction with Environmental Systems Research Institute, Inc. (ESRI) has compiled and published the Salton Sea Atlas, *a marvelously photographed and illustrated manual which dispels many myths, the most noteworthy of which is that the Sea is not terminally polluted. At least not any more than any comparable water body anywhere else in the world. This has caused developers to once again cast their eyes toward Salton City, which is less than ten percent built out on the grand plans laid by M. Penn Phillips in the early fifties.*

Noted land planner Frank Laulainen of Resort Towns International (and a main player on this development team) states that the M. Penn Phillips development saga of woe and remorse is not at all unusual. In city planning and subsequent development there are frequently "pioneers" who lay the groundwork but run out of funding before their dreams are realized. Their work benefits future developers who pick up on their seed efforts and bring them to fruition.

Salton City is on the verge of a renaissance. First, is the fact that any large body of water smack dab in the middle of the desert will eventually draw people—it's inevitable. Second, is that the well-to-do Coachella Valley communities to the north are running out of land and the prices of that which is left is skyrocketing. In comparison, Salton City land prices are still considered reasonable. Third, the Imperial County communities to the south are all experiencing a steadily increasing population growth. And fourth, the ramifications of the frequently forgotten about North American Free Trade Agreement (NAFTA) are soon to be realized. Established in 1994, NAFTA proposes to lift all barriers to free trade between Canada, the United States, and Mexico by 2009. Inhabitants of Mexicali, Mexico, less than sixty miles away, are becoming and will become wealthy overnight. They will look to nearby resort towns in which to spend their disposable income. And finally, if Congresswoman Bono's Salton Sea revitalization efforts are realized when the ballot comes up in 2008 the area will once again become a recreational Mecca.

Tom Cannell, the General Manager of the Salton Community Services District, states that over 750 building permits for houses in Salton City have been issued in the first four months of 2005. Rare is the opportunity in life to get in on the ground floor of a building boom. This is certainly one such opportunity.

I don't feel all development is bad, I feel bad development is bad. How developmental interests merge with environmental interests is a mystery to some but not to me. This is because I realize that the human population continues to grow and we are going to have to find a place to put everyone. Haphazard planning will assuredly hurt the environment more than well-planned growth although, I must admit, both will hurt the environment to some degree. My life has become a manifestation of the "lesser of two evils" theory and I console its apparent contradictions with the thought that I care deeply about the environment and therefore will keep its concerns foremost in my land planning efforts, more at least, than the other guy. Time will tell if this is true.

So, for now, I put Anza on hold as I wait to see how all the small town politics shake out against big money development interests merged with typical bullying big Republican political aspirations and fear for the very worst.

Whatever will be will be and please don't blame it on me. A prophet is never recognized in his homeland. And so I cast my lot on the shores of the Salton Sea.

Postscript

The resurrection of the Old Salton City Golf Course was wholeheartedly embraced by the Imperial County planning staff and the citizens of Salton City. Unfortunately, they are not the ones who fund development projects and this one was shortly thereafter sacrificed on the altar of greed. Investors and lenders ultimately felt that the project would fail because the housing element needed to be priced at $500,000.00 to drive the project.

The median home price in that area was $260,000.00, with $325,000.00 being the high end of the scale. Even though similar golf course community housing ran into the *multi-millions* in the Coachella Valley cities just thirty miles to the north, no one was willing to take the leap of faith necessary to view Salton City as anything but a lower-middle to middle-class community. The project died on the vine and fell out of escrow costing me about $20,000 of my own hard-earned money. Others are trying to get it off the ground and I may yet become involved on the planning/design end. Or not. So where do I cast my lot now? Stay tuned.